Prisms of Prejudice

Prisms of Prejudice

MEDIATING THE MIDDLE EAST FROM THE UNITED STATES

Karin Gwinn Wilkins

UNIVERSITY OF CALIFORNIA PRESS

University of California Press
Oakland, California

Library of Congress Cataloging-in-Publication Data

Names: Wilkins, Karin Gwinn, 1962- author.
Title: Prisms of prejudice : mediating the Middle East from the United States / Karin Gwinn Wilkins.
Description: Oakland, California : University of California Press, [2021] | Includes bibliographical references and index.
Identifiers: LCCN 2021020095 (print) | LCCN 2021020096 (ebook) | ISBN 9780520377004 (cloth) | ISBN 9780520377028 (paperback) | ISBN 9780520976368 (epub)
Subjects: LCSH: Prejudices in the press—United States. | Mass media and public opinion—United States. | Middle East—In mass media.
Classification: LCC DS62 .W49 2021 (print) | LCC DS62 (ebook) | DDC 956—dc23
LC record available at https://lccn.loc.gov/2021020095
LC ebook record available at https://lccn.loc.gov/2021020096

30 29 28 27 26 25 24 23 22 21
10 9 8 7 6 5 4 3 2 1

For my children

ALEXANDER MONROE SIEGENTHALER &

KATHERINE GRACE SIEGENTHALER

I have hope for the future because of you

Contents

Illustrations

FIGURES

TABLES

Acknowledgments

This project brings together many years of work that have contributed to this book directly as well as indirectly, through concern for and study of hate crimes, implicit bias, and humanitarian responsibility. I am indebted to and respectful of the many who have experienced and suffered prejudice. I write this during an unimaginable period of global pandemic, as well as a shift in how we witness and address injustice and inequity. We must improve communication in order to imagine, and then enact, a better world.

I want to thank the many people and agencies devoted to documenting hate crimes and fighting for better policies and practices that will direct us toward a more compassionate and fair society. One such person is James Zogby, whose work with the Arab American Institute plays a critical role in this advocacy. I want to thank Jim and his expert research team for their thoughtful and dedicated work on the national survey described in chapter 4. I thank the reviewers and editorial team from the *International Communication Gazette*, who published an earlier version of the survey analysis. I also appreciate the important work of my professional organizations, the Arab-US Association for Communication Educators (AUSACE), the International Association for Media and

Communication Research (IAMCR), and the International Communication Association (ICA).

Decades ago, fellowship support from the St. Andrew's Society enabled my initial study of Arabic at the University of Edinburgh, followed two years later by Rotary International support for a year at the American University in Cairo. These fellowships were transformational in my personal and professional life, creating the opportunity for direct experience and study that informed my perspective in a way that shaped my career as well as this book project. Investment in supporting experiences such as these serves as a critical step in building the empathy necessary to fight prejudice.

Many of my academic colleagues and friends have offered insightful and helpful suggestions throughout this process. Some of the most valuable suggestions came from confidential reviewers of this book in its early stages. Sincere thanks to Silvio Waisbord, who spoke with me early on about the overarching conceptualization articulating prejudice as mediated through a prism. Other friends reading and offering helpful suggestions include John Downing, Marwan Kraidy, Doug Boyd, and Mohammed El-Nawawy. Thanks to Amy Jordan, Nick Couldry, Cees Hamelink, and Lianne Dookie for inspiring and supporting my professional work. Running with Susan Harnden, for close to twenty years, has been instrumental in grounding my perspectives.

Over the many years of research that contributed to this project, I have worked with several students at the University of Texas at Austin and the University of Miami. From the latter, I appreciate the diligence and contributions from Michael Kim and the Orange Umbrella team, notably Alexandra Sofia Chavez Altadonna for her skill in producing visual graphics. In Austin I had the privilege to work with LaRisa Anderson, Karen Lee, Hao Cao, Ryan Wang,

Kelly Houck, Amina Ibrahim, Selena Dickey, Soyoung Park, Misa Mascovich, Sidrah Shah, Lakayla Williams, Jackie Fenson, Michael Vetter, and Jon Alexander.

I am particularly grateful to the University of California (UC) Press, for working with me on this manuscript and production. I signed on through Lyn Uhl, whose expertise and experience gave me the confidence that this project would culminate in a work of value. Thank you to Niels Hooper and Madison Wetzell at UC Press for the patient and thoughtful reviews and for shepherding this project to completion. Thank you also to Gary Hamel and BookComp professionals for thoughtful editorial suggestions.

Finally, I thank my husband, Paul Rubin, for being such a supportive partner through professional transitions and the prolonged attention that this project has absorbed. And to my children, Kari and Alex, thank you for reminding me of what matters in life and giving me hope for our future.

1 *Prisms of Prejudice*

Media do not reflect: media refract. And this matters. Established and enduring prisms of prejudice are mediated through popular culture, through news and information, and through official discourse. *Prisms of Prejudice* examines social and political constructions that articulate sentiments within the United States that have consequences not only for foreign policies and international relationships but also for the experiences of Arab and Muslim US citizens and for norms in US culture.

Prejudice in the United States against Arab and Muslim communities is increasingly evident in the proliferation of hate groups, violent incidents, negative public discourse, and restrictive public policies. Racist rhetoric and supremacist movements have emerged with more visibility and violence in recent US history. Contemporary political conflict in this country highlights crucial divides in race, ethnicity, gender, sexual orientation, class, and other distinctions that contribute to inequities in rights and resources. Protests against designated travel bans, police killings, racial inequality, restrictions on military participation, and other central concerns characterize resistance against powerful prejudices within the United States. With the rising tide of discriminatory practices and pronouncements directed particularly against Arab and Muslim communities in the United States, it is worth documenting the constructions and consequences of negative media characterizations of Islam, Arab communities, and the Middle East in general.

This project considers only one aspect of a complex set of dynamics, focusing on US articulations of and toward Arab and Muslim communities, with the recognition that these identities are distinct yet overly conflated through simplistic media narratives. Americans who identify as Muslim number over 2 million adults and an estimated 3.35 million when including children (Pew Research Center, 2017a). About 60 percent of these adults are immigrants—first-generation Americans, mostly from South Asian and Middle East–North African (MENA) regions. This is a racially and ethnically diverse group, including, among others, African Americans (24%), South Asian Americans (23%), and Arab Americans (22%) (Beydoun, 2018, p. 20). While Muslims account for only 1 percent of the US population, worldwide 12 percent of the global community aligns with Islam, constituting a majority in forty-nine countries throughout the Asian-Pacific, Middle East–North African, and Sub-Saharan regions (Pew Research Center, 2017b). Despite proselytization from some factions of Islamist terrorists, less than 1 percent of the global Muslim community affiliates with these violent groups (Kurzman, 2018), contrary to contemporary prejudicial assumptions.

Currently estimated at 3.7 million (AAI, 2017a), Arab-American communities are composed of diverse ancestries, faiths, and cultures, with an increasing solidarity emerging through political movements and advocacy organizations, such as the Arab American Institute (AAI) and the American-Arab Anti-Discrimination

Committee (ADC). Early Arab immigrants, following the fall of the Ottoman Empire prior to World War I, were mostly Christian families. Over time, Arab immigrants to the United States have come from many countries, increasingly of Muslim faith. Recent trends include more Muslim and Christian Iraqi and Syrian families, though the largest Arab-American communities identify with Lebanese and Egyptian heritage (AAI, 2017a; Semaan, 2014). These distinct histories are obscured when identities are conflated in mediated discourse.

Following a period of relative invisibility in US official discourse, when Arab Americans were designated "white" in the national census, advocacy efforts increasingly have worked toward creating more relevant and comprehensive categories, though they have not achieved official census recognition (ADC, 2017; Semaan, 2014). This advocacy is predicated on shared experiences of discrimination juxtaposed with the white privilege accorded those of European descent. Muslim, Arab, and other American communities have had their citizenship and patriotism publicly and routinely questioned in post 9/11 America, with Arab Muslim Americans experiencing more discrimination than Arab Christian Americans (Akram, 2002; Alsultany, 2012; Beydoun, 2018; Selod, 2015; Semaan, 2014).

These trends toward public prejudice have been emerging over time, with an increasing number of anti-Muslim groups documented by the Southern Poverty Law Center (2017a; 2017b), rising to 101 in 2016 from 34 in 2015, and from an even lower number of 5 in 2010. It is not just the absolute numbers of hate groups in general that are increasing. Reviewing these statistics more closely shows that the proportion of hate devoted to Muslim communities has grown from 4 percent of all US-based hate groups in 2015 (34/892), to 11 percent (101/917) in 2016. While documentation of organized groups illustrates just one facet of a more complex dynamic of prejudice, this does signify a trend toward public visibility, increasingly connected with violence. The Council on American-Islamic Relations (CAIR) has documented dramatic jumps in incidents reported directly to them following 9/11, steadily rising from about two hundred to three hundred a year in the preceding five years to one thousand by 2003 and onward, to the point of quadrupling this estimate by 2018 (Hooper, 2018). The 9/11 juncture also anticipates more reported violence against property, as well as passenger profiling. Hate crimes against Muslim and Arab Americans have increased dramatically since 2011, with a sharp increase from 2014 on (AAI, 2017b; Bridge Initiative, 2017; Beydoun, 2018; Pitter, 2017). Public acts and expressions of hate against US citizens find support through problematic media narratives that affect human relationships and social perceptions (Tukachinsky, 2015).

Mediated Prejudice

Media play a critical role in shaping our social identities as well as interactions, privileging some political positions and viewpoints over others. Assertions of hate may be inspired and reinforced through cultural norms prevalent in mediated public discourse. Dominant discourse takes shape not just from a single text, such as a film or news story, but as a cumulative avalanche of strong narratives that contribute over time to an assumed set of social expectations. Given the importance of narratives that construct discriminatory portraits of Arab and Muslim communities, in this research I consider not just one genre, but the resonance across narratives in popular culture, news, and foreign aid, each presenting a framework for articulating concerns and resolutions, collectively reinforcing problematic stereotypes. The relatively recent emergence of shared online videos is outside the scope of this project but would be a valuable extension of this work in future scholarship.

Mediated assertions of the Middle East, whether through film, broadcast news, or government policies and statements, can be considered in terms of their narratives, which typically offer simplified plots without historical context; their characters, in terms of negative and limited attributes; and their constructed maps, inscribing both boundaries and landscapes that shape action and sentiment. In this exploration of US media constructions of Arab and Muslim communities, action-adventure becomes a dominant frame, asserting empire as noble and rescue as necessary, where Middle Eastern landscapes serve as passive backgrounds for conquest and violence.

In addition to considering how US narratives in popular culture, news, and foreign aid compare across these public platforms, I consider the extent to which dominant themes may have changed over time. This historical lens is particularly critical in this study, given the projected expectation that U.S. media became more discriminatory following 9/11 in 2001. Keeping this year in mind, I question the degree to which dominant media constructions in the United States may have changed since the mid-1990s or may endure despite small fluctuations.

This approach to analysis across discourses and over time is meant to allow a more comprehensive exploration of how mediated narratives prevail or endure and their consequences. The study considers the significance of mediated narratives that contribute to a dominant "mediated construction of reality," building on Couldry and Hepp's (2017) insightful framework. Their scholarship offers a significant justification for and explanation of this theoretical direction, building on the essential work of Silverstone (2002) and Martin-Barbaro (1993), whose groundbreaking contributions to communication studies insightfully situate narrative content within national cultures. While it may be easy to focus on the consequences of media saturation, Silverstone's scholarship reminds us that mediation engages a broader "transformative process in which the meaningfulness and value of things are constructed" (2002, p. 745). He describes mediation as a "fundamentally, but unevenly, dialectic process in which institutionalized media of communication . . . are involved in the general circulation of symbols in social life" (p. 762). This approach to understanding communication, then, offers a comprehensively and contextually bound framework, recognizing that this dialectic engagement is neither smooth nor linear, given asymmetrical power dynamics.

Subsequently, Couldry (2008), Hepp (2019), Hjarvard (2013), Schulz (2004), and others (Hepp et al., 2015) have drawn attention to mediatization, emphasizing media logics as central to social transformation and political action. Hepp's (2019) description of mechanization, electrification, and digitization as waves of mediatization illustrates the importance of understanding how these logics are integral to our society, particularly as current trends toward datafication inscribe implicit biases with far-reaching consequences through the construction and assertion of particular algorithms. Central to Hepp's (2019) articulation of "deep mediatization" are key points that contribute to the theoretical foundations of this work: we understand media as a process, not solely as content or technology; as a sensitizing concept, considering how communication may shape perception beyond simplistic media effects; and as embedded in social infrastructure, considering how our practices contribute to a media repertoire of patterns.

Recognizing that mediation and mediatization are not mutually exclusive concepts, this work sees the importance of media logics and systems as integrated with other institutional practices and social norms, intending to move our focus from being exclusively on texts to considering broader consequences and contexts (Couldry & Hepp, 2013; Kunelius & Reunanen, 2016; Pamment, 2015). This project relies on mediation as a theoretical conceptualization that centers on the importance of media without overly aggrandizing technologies, moving away from a linear model of media effects toward a more holistic perspective that positions mediated texts as produced and understood through social interpretations, grounded in political contexts, and contributing to political decisions (Christensen & Peterson, 2017; Couldry, 2012; Enghel, 2016; Livingston & Lunt, 2014). Media do more than influence narrowly operationalized attitudes; media shape norms of prejudice that challenge our everyday lives.

US media work to mediate the Middle East for American audiences through articulation of Arab and Muslim communities as antithetical to projected American values. Attitudes relevant to this study consider perceptions of Arab and Muslim communities, along with others in the United States, in ways that specify interest in collaboration with the Middle East as well as fear of terrorism. In this way, preference for or against constructed cultural groups based on generalized stereotypes is considered more prevalent in the absence of direct connection and thus more susceptible to mediated stereotypes (Bell, 2017; Downing & Husband, 2005).

Situating media texts within contexts allows us to privilege the importance of politics within normative climates. In the United

States, a "war on terror" has been a central frame, used not only to build support for aggressive policies, but also to justify discriminatory practices against Arab and Muslim communities (Hatton & Nielson, 2016), migration control, and citizen surveillance (Castonguay, 2015). National policies and projects under President Trump included domestic surveillance under the guise of "countering Islamic violence," registering Muslim immigrants into the United States, creating travel bans, and restricting civic organizations and programs (Beydoun, 2018, p. 9). Invoking this prejudice builds on collective fear. Public attention to terrorism can be seen as "a product of propaganda of fear that has defined a plethora of U.S. news coverage for more than a decade" (Altheide, 2013, p. 233), through accentuating a sense of danger and offering a simplistic account of violence without context (Evans, 2010).

Through this research I intend to demonstrate the persistence and prevalence of problematic narratives projected through US media, as well as the consequences of these dominant themes to public opinion, shaping public action and public policies. Chapter 4, concerning consequences, follows chapter 3's consideration of how US film, news, and foreign aid discourses offer particular narratives that discriminate against Arab and Muslim communities. And this consideration of media narratives builds on chapter 2, which explores how media map the Middle East, bounding and projecting particular assumptions about the region and its communities.

Mapping the Middle East

Considering mediating as building upon mapping, conceptualized as an asserted construction of territory, and upon narrating, conceptualized as structuring a sequence of events guided through familiar plots and characters, chapter 2 begins by questioning basic assumptions about what constitutes the "Middle East." This is a particularly problematic articulation of complex maps, embodying multiple languages and dialects, differentiated social classes, and migrant groups, along with dominant and marginalized national communities. Most importantly for this project, the projection of "Middle" and "East" implicates the observer, viewed from the perspective of Northern and Western agencies. Another vantage point might consider this territory as "Western Asia," for example, in relation to South or East Asia. Mapping engages a power structure, through which those with resources control the parameters that limit material, economic, and human mobility.

Political mapping builds on historical assumptions as well as contemporary agendas of national and global agencies (Shah & Wilkins, 2004), which are inspired and perpetuated through mediated articulations in policies, popular culture, and news. This conceptualization of mapping stems from Gregory Bateson's (1972) work, in his explorations of how social constructions create "maps" that are distinct from "territories," representing the product of political struggles over the categorization of areas, routes, and directions with clear consequences to peoples' lives (Tawil-Souri, 2012; Wilkins, 2008; Wilkins, 2018a).

The construction of a global space referred to as the "Middle East" illustrates an outcome of mapping that embodies centuries of political imperialism. Beydoun (2018) writes that "these contiguous regions, also home to sizable non-Muslim and indigenous non-Arab populations, were consolidated into one region called the "Middle East," itself a product of Orientalist perspective, creation, and geographic ambiguity" (p. 53). Maps such as these suggest "geopolitical truth" (Dittmer, 2005) when learned as "facts," thus legitimizing the territorial boundaries as "natural" rather than as politically contested borders. Global maps delineating nation-states justify the division of complex cultural groups into seemingly neatly defined nations, despite the strength of transnational ties and the prevalence of conflict over national borders.

In this chapter I consider two broad questions concerning US media mapping: How do US government and media sources map the Middle East? and What perspectives are privileged? With reference to the first question, I consider what is visible, and by extension what is not visible through these frames. Next, I consider the shaping of a "Middle East" across various government sources. This analysis begins with attention to US government agencies with interests in the Middle East, including the Department of State (DOS), the Agency for International Development (USAID), the Central Intelligence Agency (CIA), the Federal Bureau of Investigation (FBI), the Office of the US Trade Representative (USTR), and the Department of Agriculture (DOA). The construction of the Middle East is then considered in terms of the countries included in each official jurisdiction of this territory, as well as the assignation of these countries as areas for development, trade, intervention, and other official US actions. These maps are considered in relation to historical timelines registering US intervention in the region.

While maps of the Middle East created by US agencies engaged in funding, collaboration, and combat in these territories assert explicitly political interests, the Middle East projected through public news attention implies an indirect political agenda created through recognition of events and people in the region. In this analysis, broadcast news from central television sources (ABC, CBS, CNN, and NBC) are consulted in terms of the places from which news is reported, as well as the places that become subjects of news. Differences are considered across organizational sources, as well as over time (1996–2018). Focusing on these four specific television channels allows us to consider the more mainstream sources prevalent within the United States. Television broadcast news serves as the source for this analysis, given its wider access and reach than prominent print news sources, as well as closer connection to broadcast political satire, itself a dominant source of news within the United States. Pew research identifies television as the most cited source of news among Americans, higher than reading news online or in print or than listening to the radio (Kohut et al., 2010). Particularly in terms of foreign news, studies suggest that US-based audiences are more likely to find news through entertaining, "soft" news sources, indicating the relevance of television over print (Baum, 2002).

Mapping is also considered in terms of the landscapes projected in popular films that reference the Middle East, either through the site of action or through central characters. Popular films refer to the top twenty grossing films documented each year between 1996 and 2018, focusing on those that reference the region ($n = 49$). The original sample included the year 1995, which had no relevant films for this analysis; whether we include this earlier year for a total of twenty-three or twenty-four years, roughly 10 percent of popular films are included for consideration, having some reference to the Middle East. In this analysis, I consider which countries are explicitly featured in these films, whether as urban or desert landscapes, and whether as current, future, past, or mythical in time. It is also important to note whether these landscapes offer passive scenery for actors foreign to that local context and whether the action engaged is violent. Analysis of visual images is considered in terms of the still photographs used to publicize development projects, along with central marketing images for key films and videogames identified with references to the Middle East.

These constructions are considered across the genres and sources in which the Middle East becomes figured in this conceptual mapping, as well as over time. This analysis of perspective articulated through mapping grounds the next chapter, which concerns how US media narrate the Middle East.

Narrating the Middle East

In chapter 3, I demonstrate the resonance of an action-adventure narrative, dominant in films and video games, with narratives in news and foreign aid, to explain problems, their causes, and their heroic resolutions. Given its prominence in popular culture, action-adventure is a dominant approach to structuring narratives and texts that feature the Middle East as landscape or through characters. These narratives are explored across these sources and over time. The chapter considers potential shifts in or endurance of key themes that position the Middle East as a passive landscape or an empty slate, as well as characters as weak or evil, in relation to a heroic and benevolent United States, armed with modern technologies and weapons.

The sources for this analysis include official documentation of US development assistance to the region, along with the television news transcripts and popular films described in the previous chapter. Film serves as a valuable source of data, illustrating dominant narratives in mainstream and popular media. Supplementing analyses of popular film, I include an overview of videogames. This industry has surpassed that of global film in terms of revenue (Alvarez, 2015; *The Economist*, 2011; Statistica, 2015). Even with the rise of other national film industries, the United States remains one of the top producers of global film (Crane, 2014). Film and video game industries constitute significant agents contributing to dominant narratives produced and distributed on a global scale.

Extensive scholarship on US popular culture has demonstrated the prominence of action-adventure rescue missions and mythical fantasies when plots, characters, and landscapes feature the Middle East (Alsultany, 2012, 2016; McAlister, 2005; Shaheen, 2001; Wilkins, 2008). Whether characterizing this region as an exotic fantasy or as a slate for empire, these communities and cultures are painted according to the perception of the dominant agencies constructing these narratives. The action-adventure narrative follows plots that allow heroes to resolve suspenseful conflict through winning challenging battles against evil villains on behalf of vulnerable and weak victims. McAlister (2005) references the televisual appeal of war that contributed to the spectacle of Gulf War coverage as "both a major military action and a staged media event" (p. 240) linking news narratives with those in video games. Relying on simplistic plots and brief dialogues, this genre has been remarkably profitable on a global scale, given projected accessibility, compared with drama and comedy, across cultural and linguistic boundaries.

Given the focus on US media and agencies, these analyses recognize the geopolitical interests that contribute to particular characterizations, visualized landscapes, and sequenced events (McDonald, 2014, p. 118), building on a sense of nationalist exceptionalism. Pamment (2015) identifies US geopolitical narratives as emanating from a "frontier thesis," as part of a historical imaginary that supported western expansion from the East, and toward the South in accordance with the Monroe Doctrine. The United

States becomes privileged as heroic, justified in its territorial acquisitions and its global intervention (Lubin & Kraidy, 2016). Moreover, this heroism on behalf of the nation is coded as masculine and white (Nakayama & Krizek, 1995). Although over time US heroes have been portrayed as ethnically diverse (Alsultany, 2012, p. 69; McAlister, 2005, p. 265), this projected multiculturalism mistakenly portrays these dynamics as harmonious rather than recognizing implicit racism, and still excludes Arab, Iranian, and Muslim characters in sympathetic roles (Alsultany, 2015, 2016). Instead, these latter communities conventionally comprise villain and victim roles.

A rescue fantasy values masculine heroes in their roles as saviors of vulnerable victims, who tend to be "other" women (Aguayo, 2009), particularly those who are Arab or Muslim living outside of the United States (Ahmed & Matthes, 2017; Alsultany, 2012). This obsession with rescue applies not only to people, but also to artifacts, particularly when projected as unappreciated or misunderstood in other cultures (McAlister, 2005), thus justifying intervention (Ibrahim, 2010). Whether we are considering the commodification of King Tut for traveling exhibits or for comedic ridicule on *Saturday Night Live*, or the treasures "discovered" by archeologist Howard Carter in 1922, privileging a mythical sense of Ancient Egypt, the rescue concept avoids attention to political complexities in contemporary Egypt and reinforces a sense of need for foreign intervention (McAlister, 2005).

A popular referencing of mummies and pharaohs serves both as a source of comedy, as in the Fitzwater Brigade's 2017 contribution to the New Year's Mummers Parade, as well as a source of fear, illustrated through such recent films as *The Mummy* (2017) and *Gods of Egypt* (2016). The assertion of cultural communities as derived from "magical kingdoms" assures that these narratives are devoid of contemporary political context. This narrative transcends genre, as evidenced in an episode entitled "Marrakesh" (*Somebody Feel Phil,* 2020, season 3, episode 1), when eponymous Phil explains to a local chef that "I've always wanted to come here because it, to me, it was almost like a fantasy. A place that existed, that wasn't real, to me."

Villains pose threats in this narrative, typically perceived as external to the projected home community, whether through racial or foreign status (Marchetti, 1989). Extensive research of US media documents a persistent characterization of Muslim and Arab men in these roles (Aguayo, 2009; Dittmer, 2005; Kozlovic, 2007; Morey, 2010; Shaheen, 2001; Wilkins & Downing, 2002). Exceptions include men as naive sympathizers, as in *Syriana*, or with subordinate value to central protagonists, as in *Iron Man* (Bayraktaroğlu, 2014), though these roles are rare. The threat of terrorism structures these narratives in film (Downing, 2007) and television (Morgan & Shanahan, 2017), as well as news (El-Nawawy & Elmasry, 2017; Kumar, 2014; Watson, Selod, & Kibria, 2018). This threat attributes the cause of violence to Islam (Afshar, 2013; Ahmed & Matthes, 2017; Al-Zo'by, 2015; Beydoun, 2018; Horsti, 2017), positioning this community as antithetical to projected rational and secular US values (Amin-Khan, 2012; Ekman, 2015; McAlister 2005; Morey & Yaqin, 2010).

The threat of terror aligned with a sense of helplessness among victims contributes to a construction of a justified hero, able and willing to do what must be done. This narrative accentuates public fear in order to create public support for US intervention (Downing,

2013; Ekman, 2015). Building this support requires a foundation of social norms that justify political pursuits. Enduring narratives perpetuated through varied sources and channels contribute to this mediation, considered in the next chapter.

Mediating the Middle East

In chapter 4, I question how narratives shape public attitudes. Given the saturation of dominant themes established in previous chapters, through this analysis I document the consequences of persistent and prevalent themes in US public discourse. To engage an intermediary level of consequence, between dominant narratives and contemporary debates, I rely on primary survey data, connecting affinity for action-adventure with problematic public opinions, demonstrating the importance of these media texts, particularly when people have no direct connection or experience with Muslim, Arab, or Middle Eastern communities. Through this analysis, I focus on the concerns of Arab and Muslim Americans, considering the consequences of negative media characterizations of Islam, of Arab communities, and of the Middle East. These norms contribute to the attitudes and experiences of those targeted with problematic stereotypes, perpetuating prejudice, profiling, and policies.

The word *prejudice* here refers to perceptions of Arab and Muslim communities, within the United States as well as in the Middle East, in ways that specify interest in collaboration from fear of terrorism. Attitudes are then considered as potentially constructive as well as negative. Rather than suggesting that media stereotypes create a direct causal force that affects attitudes, this research is positioned as an entry into how we might understand the primacy of dominant media narratives in shaping norms that contribute to a range of attitudes as well as discriminatory practices.

The process of mediating engages the reception and distribution of texts, negotiated and understood within social, cultural, and political contexts. The term *prism* is proposed as a metaphor that engages the complexity of media production and reception. This metaphor highlights conditions of power and marginality that contribute to perspectives manifest in creating, sharing, and interpreting mediated texts. Media effects, then, are not considered as a clear reflection through an unobscured process of transition. Instead, texts are conceptualized as being refracted, shifting directions and representations when mediated, conditioned through human action and collective negotiation.

Cultural studies scholarship has referenced hostile attitudes as a "prism" in studies of racial and gender bias, as well as Islamophobia (Johnson & Loscocco, 2015; Kaler, 2010; Rada & Wulfemeyer, 2005). Marzano (2011) positions Islamophobia as a "prism" that frames news (Marzano, 2011), joined by Werbner's (2013) consideration of a popular culture prism and Gilroy's (2012) attention to a prism that integrates fear of Islam with fear of immigration. These prisms serve political interests, recognizing that these social constructions and attitudes embody broader dynamics of power, alienation, and resistance.

Mediated prisms of collective prejudices are believed to hold significance particularly when people do not have direct experience (Tukachinsky, Masto, & Yarchi, 2015). In this study, direct experience may become relevant in terms of heritage, religious affiliation, territorial residence or citizenship, travel experiences, or other conditions. Following McAlister's (2005) thoughtful claim that in the United States people are more likely to "encounter" the Middle East through media rather than personal experience, this study offers empirical evidence of the importance of media in contributing to prisms that guide attitudes toward fellow citizens as well as foreign countries. Although through analysis we may be able to differentiate travel experience and cultural affiliation as specific indicators, we recognize the role of media as complex, not neatly dichotomizing in-person experiences from mediated ones, given the convergence of technologies and increasingly engaged interactive digital platforms that structure our learning, civic engagement, and professional lives.

Global fear rests on concern with terrorism more broadly, as a normative sentiment that serves as a set of perceived threats. These concerns may transcend other considerations (Wilkins & Downing, 2002), for example when memories of film plots (Wilkins, 2008) or of suspected criminals in news or dramas (Oliver, 1999; Rockler, 2002; Shah, 2003) register villains as Arab or Muslim even when not explicitly characterized that way in texts. Literature detailing scholarship that connects media consumption with particular attitudes is described in more detail in chapter 4. There is also emerging, relevant scholarship on the effects of mediated stereotypes on those who become the target of these problematic characterizations (Albdour, et al., 2017; Schmuck, Matthes, & Paul, 2017; Tukachinsky, Mastro, & Yarchi, 2017).

I consider these key issues through primary research based on a national survey of US adults in 2017 ($n = 1{,}416$), designed to allow comparisons contrasting Arab and Muslim Americans with other citizens in terms of their attitudes toward the Middle East, experiences and perspectives in the United States, and fear of terrorism. These analyses consider experience and interest in the Middle

East as well as self-identified heritage and religious affiliation in connection to analyses correlating media interest and experience with identified attitudes.

As expected, media engagement has a stronger connection to attitudes among respondents with no direct experience or identification with Arab or Muslim communities. Action-adventure interest specifically contributes toward identified prejudices, as well as more accentuated concerns with potential terrorism. Prejudice against fellow citizens as well as global communities appears contingent upon intensive media engagement with a genre that reinforces simplistic characterizations and plots.

Visioning from the US Prism

In the concluding chapter, trends identifying public sentiments and experiences are considered in terms of the enduring narratives documented over time and across sources, whether through popular film, news, or government documents. This discussion brings together the earlier attention to mapping through the domain of institutional and historical perspectives, with a warranted concern over documented stereotypes and prejudice.

Following this summary, I explore potential ways to counter these conditions, considering broad social and political trends as well as strategic intervention. Conditions that could shift production might include education of media professionals and support for diversity in professional positions, as well as ongoing political work to counter anti-immigration sentiments and racial and other biases. Facilitating the distribution of media created by Arab, Muslim, and other professionals may also help to fragment dominant media narratives.

The problem of prejudice requires us to do more. Although this documentation of persistent and problematic narratives identifies a serious challenge, we can work to counter these prisms of prejudice through strong programs designed to refract and shift mediated positions and social conditions. Resolving this issue is a matter of ethics and empathy, requiring collective and strategic change that will endure.

2 *Mapping the Middle East*

In this chapter, I consider the importance of perspective in shaping maps of the Middle East, asserting that visual and verbal representations emerge from political agendas. The focus of this analysis begins with the political perspectives of the US government, whose agencies determine the boundaries and sources of their interactions within a designated space they refer to as "the Middle East." I also consider maps that are accorded attention in US news reports and the visual images projected through US popular culture and official development documentation when referencing this region.

Overall, I explore how particular articulations of spatial dimensions in verbal and visual references to the Middle East prevail across sources and endure over time. With the understanding that the "map is not the territory" (Bateson, 1972), the first question considered is what becomes visible in public projections of the Middle East, and by extension, not visible. How are countries, communities, and territories highlighted through official US government agencies? How do these representations contrast with those recognized in US news? And with references in US popular culture? Finally, how do these articulations of the Middle East change over time relative to US intervention?

The initial set of questions positions how maps are shaped in connection with the particular agencies from which they emerge. First, I consider the maps used to guide US agencies' work in the Middle East. These agencies include the Central Intelligence Agency (CIA), Congressional Research Service, Federal Bureau of Investigation (FBI) overseas offices, Library of Congress, Office of US Trade, US Agency for International Development (USAID), US Army, US Department of Agriculture, US Department of State, and the US–Middle East Partnership Initiative (MEPI). I then consider the construction of the Middle East in terms of the countries included in each official jurisdiction of that territory as well as the funding the US allocates to nations in the region. How countries within the region become recognized is explored through the development discourse explaining US programs.

The next set of analyses focuses on the territories and positions recognized in US news coverage when referencing the "Middle East." This discussion is based on analyses of television broadcast news (ABC, CBS, CNN, and NBC), allowing comparisons across organizational sources and over time. With this set of data, I consider the frequency of the places from which news originates, as well as places referenced directly in the news. The 7,299 news items reviewed were accessed through the Vanderbilt Television News Archive, limiting stories to those designated "evening" and "news" and including the term *Middle East* between 1996 and 2018; these data are used to assess frequency of attention over time. From the list focusing on news between 1996 and 2018, a sample was selected through a systematic random sampling process for more detailed analysis ($n = 679$). The year 1996 was selected as a starting point in order to be able to consider trends prior to 9/11. The list of all stories was produced on pages with twenty links per page: using systematic random sampling procedures, the second (#2) and eleventh (#11) on each page was then downloaded for more extensive coding. Coders were trained to record manifest-level content, with reliability estimates all well over a standard 70 percent. This analysis includes considerations of origin of story, countries referenced, and subjects addressed.

Another set of data builds from analyses of popular film. First, the twenty most popular films in the United States were listed for each year between 1996 and 2018. Films were screened to identify those with any visual or verbal reference to the Middle East. Those identified as such were then coded more extensively by seven coders who were trained to record information about the settings, plots, and central characters. To focus on mapping, I consider where the scenes referencing the Middle East are set, in terms of space and time, and whether these urban or desert backgrounds work passively as scenery or become integrated through characters' identities or actions.

Analyses of visual images bring together official photographs from USAID websites with marketing images of the relevant films referenced above. To supplement the marketing images in these popular films, I include marketing images devoted to video games that reference the Middle East as well. These games were identified from lists of the top five best-selling games since 2005; given the relatively more recent emergence of gaming as an industry, this data set does not go back earlier in time. The games were reviewed to see if any included relevant characters, plots, or settings. A total of thirty-four of the seventy (five per year from 2005 to 2018) were identified, and marketing images were collected for this analysis.

Finally, I contrast all these projections of the Middle East, articulated through mapping by US agencies, news, and popular culture, to determine what themes prevail. I consider similarities as well as differences, distinguishing shifts in patterns over time, to identify enduring maps. Historical dynamics between the United States and other nations in this region inform these analyses.

Mapping as Perspective

The underlying issue of mapping is that a particular perspective becomes privileged in this articulation. "East" clearly situates the observer with a western perspective, as has been identified frequently in discussions of Orientalism (Said, 1978), initiated through European and British historical engagement as well as that of the United States (Said, 1997). "Middle" then references a broader geographical range and situates the region within its proximate neighbors. Within this geographical context, the referenced "Middle East," as a category meant to depict a region, oversimplifies the varied cultures, languages, and dialects that exist among its communities, which are broadly divergent in terms of access to economic resources and global mobility.

Curti (2011) devotes a special issue of *Aether: The Journal of Media Geography* to this very discussion, recognizing the focused attention of the news media and popular culture on the "Middle East's" conflicts and resources. The "geographical imagination" of this construction essentializes and oversimplifies representations of varied "ethnic, linguistic and cultural spaces" (Curti, 2011, p. 2). These particular aspects of prejudice in turn contribute to a collective normative framework that guides discourse.

While the term *Middle East* is prevalent in US public discourse, from a different vantage point, the same area could be categorized in other ways, for example, *western Asia*, as the United Nation

Economic and Social Commission for Western Asia designates it.[1] Some articulations of the Middle East include the Maghreb, a collection of northern and western countries extending through Mauritania to join Algeria, Libya, Morocco, and Tunisia in the Arab Maghreb Union; other conceptualizations emphasizing Muslim affinities extend to include Pakistan. This diversity of conceptualization contributes to a kaleidoscope of patterns made visible through the prisms of institutional assertions.

The term *Middle East* is also used in languages other than English, such as the Portuguese *Oriente Médio*, used in both Brazil and Portugal.[2] And "中东" is used in China.[3] Similar to words used in the British *Near East* and French to *Proche Orient*, the Russian script Ближний Восток / blizhniy vostok translates as "Near East," with related cognates of the first term implying proximate military connection and the second implying social connection, not location. Downing finds this depiction of the region as "east" to be odd, given that its geographical location is south of western Russia.[4] And the translated terms for this region in Mandarin and Portuguese have less to do with the location of the area relative to the observing nation than with resonant terms in the dominant language and historical perspective of northern and western elites.

Although *Middle East* has become common usage across regions and in a variety of geographic locations despite their positioning to the north, west, or other orientation, it is important to recognize that the term is less than a century old (Koppes, 1976). Culcasi (2010) explains that its use is rooted in British imperialist naval expeditions to India, which considered Turkey as "near," and China as "far." Although other regional areas are demarcated by continental names such as "Africa," "Europe," and "Asia," this region remains known by an imperialist vision inspired by merchants and military missions. The United States began to use this demarcation in its foreign policy with the advent of the Cold War, even though its definition lacked clear contours or consensus (Davison, 1960). Over time, this term became associated in the United States with values antithetical to the American way of life, with incessant conflict and crisis, or as a site of mystery (Culcasi, 2010). This construction of the "Middle East" unfortunately remains prevalent.

The power to name geographical territories belongs to those able to monopolize the production of knowledge through verbal and visual mapping. Although historically and conceptually there are serious disparities over this articulation, mapping has been used to construct this region for a variety of institutional purposes. A recent exhibition at the Blanton Museum of Art (June–August 2019) in Austin, Texas, explores "space and history in 16th-century Mexico" through the framework of "mapping memory," illustrating the importance of perspective in constructing and interpreting official accounts of expeditions and conquests. These are political maps, articulating assumptions about cultures and communities within the described area (Bateson, 1972; Wilkins, 2009). Considered as "geopolitical truth" (Dittmer, 2005), maps are more often memorized as facts than seen as contested, though over time documented boundaries shift with political transitions and military conquests. These boundaries can impede as well as structure the mobility of people and products (Tawil-Souri, 2012). Mapping privileges the perspectives of those with power through asserting boundaries and foregrounding connections in foreign aid and intervention, news coverage, and popular culture.

This positioning of mapping focuses on the hegemonic dominance of those agencies able to assert their constructions, while recognizing the possibility of resistance explored in recent scholarship concerning participatory mapping (Nossek & Carpentier, 2019; Voniati, Doudaki, & Carpentier, 2018). Proposed as a methodological approach relying on multiple data sources, this valuable process considers organization of knowledge given boundaries enacted through community and alternative media. Distinct from this consideration of community practice, the study here situates mapping as a construction produced through the work of dominant agencies.

Geopolitical power, then, serves those who dominate on a global scale, shaping the world around them through creating and engaging categories of difference. Shah and Wilkins (2004) illustrate this dynamic referencing as a "geometry of development," whereby categories such as "north" and "south," "east" and "west," "first" and "third worlds" are articulated as conventional wisdom. The term *third world* used by wealthier countries positions "them" as requiring development assistance from a privileged "us," clearly fitting this discussion of the United States as a significant global agent (Escobar, 1995; Nederveen Peterse, 2001) that asserts its constructions of the world through its policies, news, and film.

Constructions of the Middle East have a particular history within the United States, understanding the region as a target of development assistance and military intervention. Lerner's (1958) classic text has been singled out as emblematic of an Orientalist approach to development work in the Middle East (Said, 1978; Shah, 2011; Wilkins, 2004). Despite prominent and consistent critiques in the academic community regarding the patriarchal, xenophobic, and simplistic character of this model of social change, the dominant themes articulated in Lerner's model live on in current public discourse in the United States concerning development

(Escobar, 1995; Shah, 2011; Wilkins, 2004). US intervention in the Middle East may be seen as an assertion of "empire," explained by Sassan (2006) as a dynamic engaged by sovereign states in their reliance on soft power to support dominant political geographies that benefit the United States (McAlister, 2005). Makdisi (2016) agrees, determining that: "Nowhere else in the world are the power, stakes and nature of the US empire today more obvious than in the Middle East" (p. 206). The assertion of empire also takes on more direct forms, as foreign aid and interventions are employed to reward allies and punish errant states.

Given the focus of this project on the United States as a central agent within global dynamics, it is worth noting how McAlister (2005) repeatedly references the "moral geographies" asserted by the United States, which describes itself "as an island of liberty in a sea of danger. The danger, it was understood, came from Muslims, and in the post-9/11 climate, "radical Islam" developed racial overtones" (p. 302). Moreover, this "powerful mapping fused Islam, the Middle East, and terrorism" (p. 302). In this global mapping, the United States is positioned as the central and significant hero against a constructed distant and dangerous Middle East. Popular culture serves as a powerful reference for asserting these geopolitical agendas (Anaz & Purcell, 2010; Dittmer, 2005). The maps manifested through the work of US agencies are considered next, in preparation for analysis of mapping through US news and film media.

US Agencies Mapping the Middle East

In this section I consider how US national agencies shape this region through their definitions of the Middle East, their locations and program implementation, and their development assistance and military intervention. This type of attention is considered in terms of the themes of development assistance and international connection enacted. US government definitions and descriptions are contrasted to discern their different configurations, as well as to highlight what becomes distinct from what remains hidden.

Through different configurations, the "Middle East" presented by the United States might include countries across northern Africa (Morocco, Tunisia, Algeria, Libya, and Egypt), the Levant (which may refer to Iraq, Syria, Lebanon, Cyprus, parts of Turkey, Israel, Jordan, and Palestine; or more broadly a range of communities from Greece to Egypt); members of the Gulf Cooperation Council (GCC; such as Bahrain, Kuwait, Oman, Qatar, Saudi Arabia, United Arab Emirates [UAE]), as well as countries farther east including Afghanistan and Pakistan (included in the region known as MENAP, meaning Middle East, North Africa, Afghanistan and Pakistan) and others, such as Iran and Yemen (in the region but not GCC members), that do not fit neatly into these other categorizations. It is important to note that some countries can be considered in more than one category, so these are not mutually exclusive frames.

Defining the Middle East

US agencies serving as public resources offer definitions of the region that guide access to publications. The US Library of Congress refers to this constellation of countries as part of a "Near East" section of a broader "African and Middle East Reading Room."[5] The U.S. Government Printing Office organizes its publications of resources concerning "international and foreign affairs" through a category entitled "Middle East," explained as follows: "For this category we are using the broader definition of a Greater Middle East, which is a political geographic term used since at least 1980 to refer to the *traditional* Middle East such as Saudi Arabia, Kuwait and Iraq with the addition of several nearby countries, specifically Iran, Turkey, and Afghanistan. Various North African and Central Asian countries are sometimes also included. The Greater Middle East is sometimes referred to as '*The New Middle East*.'"[6] Although the explanation above has been posted on its website for at least a few years (referenced in 2016 and again in 2019), US embassies in the "Middle East" have shifted from recent inclusion of countries in North Africa (Algeria, Egypt, Libya, Morocco, Tunisia) to their categorization as part of the African region.[7] This listing of Middle Eastern presence currently includes offices in Afghanistan and the Ukraine, added to sustained embassy work in Bahrain, Jordan, Kuwait, Lebanon, Oman, Qatar, Saudi Arabia, Syria, United Arab Emirates, and Yemen.

The Office of the US Trade Representative (see Figure 1), devoted to "The United States' trade and investment relations with the countries of the Middle East and North Africa (MENA)," projects their "value in terms of both U.S. commercial and foreign policy interests." Free trade agreements with Bahrain, Israel, Jordan, Morocco, and Oman are applauded, in addition to explicitly engaged work in Algeria, Egypt, Iran, Iraq, Kuwait, Lebanon, Libya, Qatar, Saudi Arabia, Syria, Tunisia, UAE, and Yemen.

The US Department of State has shifted its categorization of this area to a "Bureau of Near Eastern Affairs," listing its active engagement in Algeria, Bahrain, Egypt, Iran, Iraq, Israel, Jordan, Kuwait, Lebanon, Libya, Morocco, Oman, Palestinian Territories, Qatar, Saudi Arabia, Syria, Tunisia, United Arab Emirates, and Yemen. In contrast to USAID's focus on development assistance, the State Department mission emphasizes security concerns, describing its regional focus on "Iraq, Middle East peace, terrorism and weapons of mass destruction, and political and economic reform."[8]

This emphasis on "national security" is reinforced through the identified mission of the CIA as: "collecting intelligence that matters, producing objective all-source analysis, conducting effective covert action as directed by the President, and safeguarding the secrets that help keep our Nation safe."[9] Notable in the CIA's list of countries comprising the "Middle East" are the countries of Armenia, Azerbaijan, and Georgia, in addition to Bahrain, Gaza Strip, Iran, Iraq, Israel, Jordan, Kuwait, Lebanon, Oman, Qatar, Saudi Arabia, Syria, Turkey, UAE, West Bank, and Yemen. Recognizing the competitive constitutions of the CIA with the FBI (Wright, 2006), these agencies share a focus on national security. The stated FBI mission is to "protect the American people" from "terrorist attack," as well as "foreign intelligence operations and espionage" and various forms of "crime." The countries of the "Middle East" they describe serving in include Afghanistan, Bahrain, Egypt, Iraq, Jordan, Kuwait, Lebanon, Oman, Palestinian National Authority, Qatar, Pakistan, Saudi Arabia, Syria, UAE, and Yemen. Subsequently, they have included Oman in its list of FBI offices, which are also in Afghanistan, Egypt, Iran, Iraq, Israel, Kuwait, Lebanon, Saudi Arabia, and Yemen (see Figure 1).[10]

The work of US public agencies in the region can be broadly defined in terms of programs identified as part of foreign aid and development, economic trade, and conflict. These are not neatly isolated categories, however. USAID states its mission in this region thus: "The American people, through USAID, support the people of the Middle East and North Africa as they strive for peace and prosperity. USAID responds to needs in the region by promoting inclusive economic growth, improving education and healthcare, supporting local democratic processes, strengthening civil society and addressing cross-border issues including water scarcity and the regional impact of conflict."[11] The foreign agricultural service similarly references these multiple goals in describing its work in Bahrain, Iran, Iraq, Israel, Jordan, Kuwait, Lebanon, Oman, Palestinian Territories, Qatar, Saudi Arabia, Syria, UAE, and Yemen.[12]

US federal agencies tend to include in their maps the five countries across northern Africa, often referred to as the "Middle East North Africa," or MENA, in their representations of the region, particularly in discussions of development. This area is highlighted in official maps and definitions produced by the US Department of State, in discussions of its regional work as well as the US Middle East Partnership Initiative; the US Office of Trade; the US Department of Agriculture; the US Library of Congress; and the US Agency for International Development (USAID) (although this agency does not include Algeria; see Figure 1). Other agencies with offices in this region tend to place them in Egypt (such as the FBI).

While countries across northern Africa tend to attract US attention from agencies dedicated to diplomacy, trade, and foreign aid, countries in the Gulf are engaged differently. The US Department of State, the Office of the US Trade Representative, the Library of Congress, the CIA, and the Department of Agriculture include six (Kuwait, Oman, Qatar, Saudi Arabia, UAE, and Yemen) of these countries in their map of the region. In contrast to this broad inclusion, USAID focuses its work in Yemen, given its mission of development assistance. Conflict in Yemen is addressed through USAID programs in the areas of health, water, education, governance, and economic growth. When describing economic programs, they include attention to "agricultural productivity and entrepreneurship" (USAID, 2015l).

Mapping countries in the Levant raises complex issues regarding contested boundaries of Palestinian communities in the West Bank and Gaza, as well as the inclusion of Israel. The US Department of State includes Israel along with Jordan, Lebanon, the West Bank, and Gaza, as does the US Department of Agriculture, the CIA, and the Office of the US Trade Representative. USAID focuses on Iraq, Jordan, Lebanon, Syria, West Bank, and Gaza in its work (until recently, with US decisions to reduce aid to Palestinian territories). USAID does not list Israel specifically in its list of countries populating the "Middle East" page.[13] However, this country becomes visible through the agency's regional programs and through a caption on a page devoted to one of these programs, referring to an "Arab Israeli olive farmer."[14]

Extending the "Middle East" to include Pakistan and Afghanistan tends to fall within the purview of those agencies devoted to conflict, such as the FBI, and the Congressional Research Service's division of Foreign Affairs, Defense and Trade. Afghanistan but not Pakistan warrants inclusion in this category by the US army's map, extending to other territories in central Asia, such as Kazakhstan and Tajikistan. The Library of Congress also includes countries in central Asia in its "Near East" section. Turkey is included in these maps of the Middle East when the FBI is considering "criminal enterprises" in the region and through the broadly defined region considered by the Library of Congress and the CIA.

Across these agencies, maps differ in terms of the degree to which they are narrowly or broadly defining the region, as well as which countries within areas become recognized through their

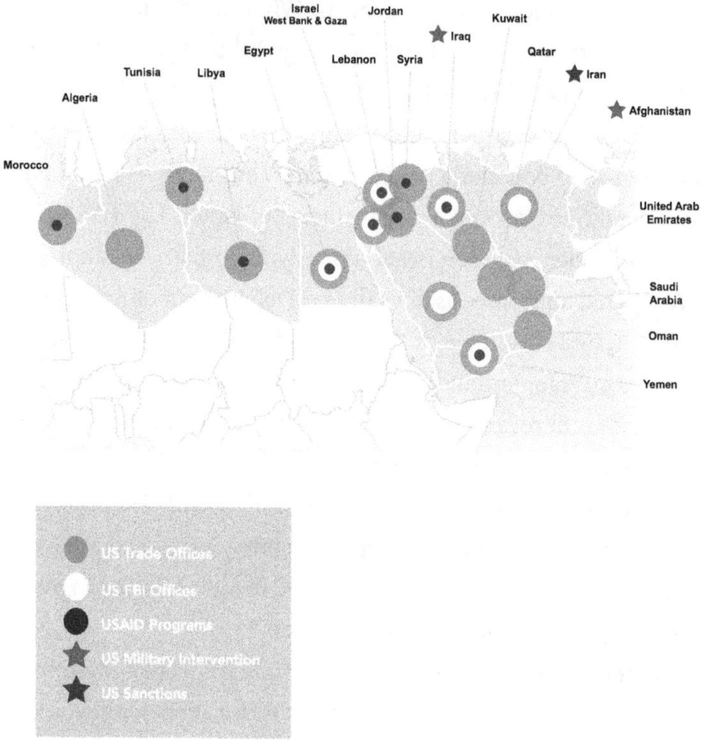

FIGURE 1. Map of US intervention in the Middle East. Graphic by Alexandra Chavez. Sources: Free Vector Maps

work. Those engaged with diplomacy and trade tend to include broader maps of the Middle East and include Israel in their representations of the region. Israel is included in a portfolio of development assistance, despite its relative wealth compared with proximate communities and countries. Other USAID work is more focused on particular countries that have official relationships with the United States and have fewer national resources than some of their neighbors in the Gulf.

It is worth considering not only where US agencies work and what countries officially become designated in this region, but also the specific funding allocated to these as recipients of foreign aid, military spending, and other forms of assistance. The next discussion summarizes foreign aid in terms of US intervention in MENA, the Levant, the Gulf, and other proximate countries.

Investing in the Middle East

US intervention in the Middle East demonstrates a willingness to employ direct military combat as well as to invest in development programs. The intensity of US interest in the region can be seen as tied to economic interests depending on concentrated regional resources, political affections and adversities with national governments, social affiliations with (and prejudices against) religious and other groups, and cultural ties with migrant and refugee communities. Development and military interventions are not easily separated in terms of programs and funding, so these US expenditures over time will be combined when considering funding to specific countries and regions.

The countries receiving the most overall funding include Afghanistan, Iraq, and Israel by far, with Egypt, Jordan, and Pakistan accorded more than other countries in 2017. U.S. foreign aid to MENA can be considered through allocations that incur obligation, notably US$19,613,271,209 in 2017, or through its actual disbursements (US$17,054,999) being less than promised.

Northern Africa has been a consistent target for US development over time, and more recently the backdrop to compelling narratives of youth resisting aging male authorities through expert use of social media (Wilkins, 2004; 2012). USAID programs channel resources to Arab countries in North Africa, particularly within modernization frames. Morocco is described as "one of America's oldest friends in the Middle East and North Africa" (USAID, 2015h). USAID missions in Libya and Tunisia (USAID, 2015j) profess interests in building democratic institutions and economic growth. In Libya media organizations are explicitly targeted for funding as a way to promote democracy as well (USAID, 2015e). These northern African countries are characterized as requiring U.S. aid to support younger generations, portrayed as "modern" and "technologically adept," to succeed older, more "traditional" people and customs, resonating clearly with a simplistic distinction epitomized in the work of development (Wilkins, 2004).

The Levant attracts resources as a way of addressing conflict and humanitarian crises, though Lebanon and Jordan have also become characterized as "modern" and "entrepreneurial" (USAID, 2015d). Jordan is valued by the US as a "voice for moderation, peace and reform in the Middle East" (USAID, 2015c). Humanitarian concerns with refugees justify funding to communities within and migrating from Syrian, Lebanese, and Palestinian territories, though the amounts and directions of this funding changes historically with US leadership and regional conflicts. For example, in 2014 the US government agreed to add US$500 million "to help those affected by the (Syrian) conflict" (USAID, 2015i), but attitudes toward and support of various refugee communities have diverged from this previous path in recent years.

Israel features not only as a major recipient of US aid, but also as partnering with the U.S. government through foreign assistance programs to Egypt, Jordan, and Palestinian authorities. Israel's prominence in the US approach to the region as a whole is also evidenced in the Middle East Regional Cooperation Program (MERC)

(USAID, 2015g), in which Israel is described as having "a vibrant scientific community," that is tasked with working collaboratively with "Arab scientists in the Middle East and North Africa [who] are using science and technology to overcome core development challenges" (USAID, 2015g). Israel also is included in the US Department of State's US–Middle East Partnership Initiative (MEPI), designed to support "organizations and individuals in their efforts to promote political, economic, and social reform in the Middle East and North Africa."[15] In these presentations Israel becomes privileged more as a partner than infantilized as a development recipient.

It is difficult to disentangle US funding to Iraq and Afghanistan, given the many agencies involved in different ways. USAID programs in Iraq have focused on "economic and agricultural growth, and help the various levels of government better represent and respond to the needs of the Iraqi people" (USAID, 2015b). Development in these areas is closely aligned with the work of military agencies.

Whereas US intervention in Iraq and Afghanistan highlight visibility in terms of rescue, given the conflicts there, other portrayals of development focus on this exchange as necessary "help" because of an assumed inability to create or sustain resources. Whether constructed as help or rescue, these motivations fit with a justification of empire as providing social benefits. The few countries that may be deemed partners through economic trade, such as Israel and Saudi Arabia, are valued in terms of their contribution to and connection with global capital.

US News Mapping the Middle East

In this section, I explore mapping implied through US broadcast television news for stories in which the key term *Middle East* appears. This sample includes news items broadcast through CNN (38% of the four television sources), which tends to be more likely to cover politics (78%) and less likely to cover violence (53%) than the other broadcast channels considered. Comparatively CNN devoted twice as much attention to the region than ABC (21%), CBS (22%), and NBC (19%). Overall, most of this television news coverage featured political issues (73%) or violence (58%), with much less recognition of cultural (3%) or economic (3%) concerns.

Across the years recorded, the most frequently referenced communities within the region were Israeli (50%) and Palestinian (46%), with this attention more likely to focus on violence (64% and 50% respectively) than coverage of other areas.[16] Moreover, when stories were not originating in North America, they were likely to be posted from offices in Israeli (22%) and Palestinian territories (11%), while occasionally from Lebanon (4%), Egypt (2%), or Iraq (2%). CNN was more likely to report from North American sites than the other stations, but also did devote more stories to the region than did the others documented. Other countries recognized in US news, though much less frequently (not exceeding 10% of the news stories), include Syria, Iran, Jordan, Saudi Arabia, Turkey, and Yemen. The region of the Levant overall features more considerably than MENA or the Gulf areas.

It is important to note that these stories must have used the term *Middle East* to count in this study. While this limitation certainly means that these analyses do not reflect *all* stories about Israel, Egypt, and other communities and nations of the region, this focus does allow us to discern which groups are most likely to surface when the region is explicitly referenced under this rubric.

The headlines and abstracts from these news reports ($n = 679$) contributed to additional analysis that considered how named countries were mapped in relation to other countries in the region and world, and how these countries gained attention. NVIVO was used to supply frequencies of words used in headlines in relation to the "Middle East," specifically noting countries, communities, and subjects. In addition, the Linguistic Inquiry and Word Count (LIWC, Pennebaker, Boyd, Jordan, & Blackburn, 2015) was used to assess psychometric properties of the words used in these news abstracts.

How the news headlines and abstract summaries reference other countries, communities, and themes contributes to our mapping of the region. When referencing the "Middle East," the most frequently referenced communities in the full television transcripts include Israelis (50%) and Palestinians (47%); when focusing only on the news abstracts, these remain the most frequently cited communities (37% and 33%, respectively).

In light of the attention accorded specific communities and subjects in relation to the broader category of the Middle East, I consider next how the countries mentioned most frequently are associated explicitly with other communities and subjects. The connections drawn in relation to others in the region are chronicled in Table 1.

Given the dominance of Palestinian and Israeli coverage and the intensive violence featured, it is not surprising that coverage of Israel includes that of Palestinians (88%) and that of Palestinian issues references Israel (63%). Inclusion of Israel is also prominent in news coverage of Turkey (78%), Egypt (47%), Lebanon (40%), Jordan (26%), and Iran (23%), with similar patterns in these countries being associated with Palestinian issues in their coverage as well. Lebanon and Syria are connected in this news coverage, as are these countries in relation to Egypt and Jordan, signifying their proximate geographical relationship in the region. Although

TABLE 1. Frequency of Association in Television News Abstracts

	Egypt %	Iran %	Iraq %	Israel %	Lebanon%	Palestine%	Syria %
Egypt	100	10	8	31			
Iran		100	16	23	7		9
Iraq	15	13	100	14			24
Israel	47	23	14	100	40	63	17
Jordan	18			26			15
Lebanon		10		14	100		44
Palestine	50	13	16	88	18	100	
Syria		13	12	5	15		100
US Pres Bush	15		18		8	8	
US Pres Clinton	18						
US Pres Obama	12	10					12
US Sec Rice					7		9
Violence	12			17	7	14	
Attack		20		19	10	8	
War			22	6	7		
Peace	26		8	15		13	
Refugees							9
Total N	34	30	50	236	60	293	34

analyses considered each named country or territory separately, in Table 1 I document cases in which at least 30 of the 679 abstracts include specific mention of these names.

It is worth noting the presence of the United States in this coverage as well, particularly in coverage of Egypt, Turkey, and Saudi Arabia. Almost half of the news associated with Egypt includes accumulated references to President Clinton (18%), President Bush (15%), or President Obama (12%), while coverage of Saudi Arabia mentions President Bush (19%) and President Obama (10%). President Bush figures prominently in coverage of Iraq, not surprising given US military intervention at the time, while President Obama is integrated in stories of Turkey (33%), Syria (12%), and Iran (10%). Words connotating violence, including *attack*, and *bombing*, were most often used in coverage of Israeli (38%) and Palestinian (33%) events, whereas the more specific term *war* was used more often with reference to Iraq (22%).

The United States serves as a central point of reference in this perspective, particularly given that most of the stories produced about the region originate within the country, as is expected in international coverage. In addition to each story's point of origin, I consider the people featured in news stories, including the presenting journalists (43%), directly quoted and featured sources (12%), quoted but not shown sources (25%), and described but not quoted news sources (20%). Most (77%) of the journalists are male and from North American (59%) or European (41%) regions. While it is not surprising that just under half of all people featured through visual or verbal referents are the journalists reporting these stories, it is important to note that most of the other informants quoted or considered come from a government agency or a nongovernmental organization.

Other voices include those who are interviewed directly and shown on screen (12%), those who are quoted but not shown (25%), and those referenced but not quoted (20%), with each step distancing the speaker from direct representation in the narrative. Among the sources contributing to these stories, a high proportion are male journalists (90%), with most aligned with North American (35%), Israeli (28%) and Palestinian (22%) communities. Far fewer voices emanate from Europe (4%), Egypt (2%), Saudi Arabia (2%), Iran (1%), Jordan (1%), or Lebanon (1%).

To consider these voices in more depth, fifteen news abstracts were randomly selected, then backgrounds on each of the forty-two individuals named in these stories, other than hosting journalists, were documented. As expected, the most frequently recognized actors in these stories were American politicians (33%), along with American military and other officials (14%). People referenced from the region include Palestinian politicians (10%), Israeli politicians (7%), Iraqi politicians (5%), Syrian politicians (5%), and Lebanese politicians (5%), as well as those from Jordan (2%) and Saudi Arabia (2%).

The tendency to rely on US official perspectives is not surprising, but it is worth noting that most of the others given voice in these news stories are politicians, usually those from countries with violence relevant to US agencies. US popular culture also constructs the region through particular perspectives, as shown in the next section.

US Film Mapping the Middle East

The Middle East is featured in US popular film as part of a cultural geography articulated through visual references. This analysis begins with considering which films among the top twenty most popular films that were initially screened in each year between 1996 and 2018 include Middle Eastern settings and landscapes.

Within the sample of relevant films ($n = 49$), representing about 10 percent of the top twenty per year, about 40 percent ($n = 19$) included the region as one of the central landscapes, and another 40 percent ($n = 19$) in which they were a relatively minor setting. Overall then, most of the films that reference the Middle East do so visually as background. Most of the settings that do so in a more central way reference Egypt, such as *The English Patient*, *Prince of Egypt*, *Mummy*, *Mummy Returns*, and *GI Joe*. Iraq also figures into these compositions, in films such as *American Sniper*. The few other areas referenced visually in central ways include Afghanistan, Dubai, Israel, Istanbul, Jerusalem, and Somalia. Minor settings, including landscape compositions in a few scenes within the overall film, again mostly reference Egypt with visions of pyramids, but also include scenes positioned as being in Afghanistan, Algeria, Dubai, Istanbul, Jordan, Morocco, and Persia or Iran (at times identifying with cities and other times as countries). It's worth noting the gendered composition of these scenes, accentuating landscapes with veiled women and robed men, for example in *X Men: Apocalypse* (2016). Also, at times visual compositions of empty desert landscapes are included with no reference to a city or country, such as *Iron Man 3*, which research coders assumed to connect to the Middle East.

The most minimal references to the Middle East region are simply emblematic symbols, such as pyramids, occupying part of its landscape. Also in these landscapes, about half of the films include signs in Arabic, providing a visual reference to position the landscape within the region. These landscapes usually are set in beige deserts (74%) rather than gray urban (26%) settings. These tend to serve as passive backgrounds against which actions take place. The more recent *Men in Black: International* (2019) offers a compelling example, explicitly situating key scenes in "Marrakesh," which serves as a site of action with minor characters as context, but the central characters and summoned heroes come from the London and New York offices (although a "North African" office is referenced, they are not called in to help). In the next section, we explore how visual references of the region are used in official agency and public culture marketing copy.

Imaging the Middle East

Perceptions of the Middle East can be discerned in the images that are used to construct visual compositions. Building from previous analyses of USAID attention to the region, I first consider the photographs used within these public pages that are meant to demonstrate US engagement in development assistance. These images offer a useful contrast to the public marketing images used in US film and video games that have been identified as referencing Middle Eastern characters or narratives. Given a broad construction of mapping as asserting visual references and reasons, next I consider these visual images.

USAID Images

An analysis of the images featured on USAID websites under the umbrella heading "the Middle East" illustrates how visual images enhance these verbal descriptions. The thirty-six photographs used for analysis include images downloaded in 2018.[17] They were produced, according to their captions, between 2013 and 2018, though most (61%) came from the more recent two years. The locations cited include Afghanistan ($n = 3$), Egypt ($n = 4$), Iraq ($n = 3$), Jordan ($n = 4$), Lebanon ($n = 4$), Libya ($n = 3$), Morocco ($n = 3$), Syrians in various locations ($n = 3$), Tunisia ($n = 3$), West Bank and Gaza ($n = 3$), and Yemen ($n = 3$). In accordance with the objectives of the agency, these images were dominated by "youth" in activities related to democratic transition, refugees and farmers appreciating or cultivating agriculture and water, women engaged in scientific testing and learning new information and communication technologies, girls in educational settings, and various compositions in support of economic growth. The photos' captions most frequently directed our attention to programs concerning agriculture (19%), governance and democracy (17%), education (17%), and women's concerns (17%), followed by attention to economic growth and tourism (11%), and access to clean water (11%). Some of these images highlighted the role of science and technology when describing food and agriculture, as well as maternal health; the importance of the private sector was also raised in some of these descriptions as well, particularly in terms of Information and Communication Technologies (ICT) industries (12%).

Most of the images (94%) depicted people (the other two portraying fruit and a landscape). The most frequently used composition included women and girls (36%) without men: these images accompanied projects addressing women's empowerment, agriculture, refugees, education, economic growth, and ICT skills. The only women to be named in the captions were those employed by USAID, and the "First Lady" of Afghanistan. Otherwise girls and women were referred to as "students," "youth," and "refugees," sometimes with their first names noted. One of the photographs of a refugee was summarized in its URL caption by "success-stories/happy-to-be-alive."

Photographs featuring only men (25%) also accompanied projects devoted to agriculture, economic growth, and citizen participation, and they were named when holding official political positions (such as minister of public health). The few photographs including both men and women (14%) positioned a male teacher lecturing to female students (described as "adolescent girls"), men sitting in a row in front of women, and a USAID female official shaking hands with farmers. Some of the photographs (22%) included both boys and girls, often described as "students" or "youth," learning entrepreneurial skills and civic engagement or pursuing other educational goals.

This small sample of official images tends to foreground people who are seen as happily and appreciatively benefitting from development; they rely on gendered constructions and accentuate the promise of youth. Much less attention is paid to donors or officials, who remain outside of the visual scope of these compositions. In contrast, images from US popular culture are more likely to highlight heroes.

Popular Culture Images

Visual images in popular culture resonate with broader constructions of the relationship between the United States and the region, privileging positions that work to justify conquest and acquisition. In this section, I consider how images used in marketing popular films and video games assert visual references.

One successful video game featuring the Middle East is *Call of Duty*, which has been produced in various manifestations (such as *Black Ops*, *Ghosts*, *Advanced Warfare*) and across platforms (mostly x360 and some ps3); several editions of *Battlefield* also were included in the analysis. Other games included *Army of Two* (2008); *Assassin's Creed* (2007); *AC Revelations* (2011); *Prince of Persia* (2008); *Spec Ops* (2012); *Splinter Cell* (2013); *Trouble in Terrorist Town* (2010); *Tomb Raider* (2007); and *Uncharted* 2 (2009). These games tend toward first-person or third-person combat scenarios across historical and contemporary settings. Iraq is the most prominently featured specific country in which current conflicts are set (*Army of Two*, *Battlefield 3*, *Splinter Cell*), while other games situate action in Afghanistan, Iran, Dubai, and Istanbul. In contrast to these contemporary settings, about one-half of these games rely on fictitious or historical settings, such as Jerusalem, Damascus, Constantinople, Egypt, and Persia.

For this analysis, we identified still visual images ($n = 34$) associated with the public marketing of each of these games. The images overwhelmingly referenced combat, with three situating their messages in mythical frames (such as a female silhouette for *Tomb Raider: Ascension*; and a male portrait for *Prince of Persia*), and only one portraying a street scene with men and women, all heads covered, and a mosque in the background. The dominant motif of conflict juxtaposed men with army helmets or occasionally sporting a symmetrical Coptic cross, against those with berets, kufiyahs, and sunglasses, with a mosque in the background or Arabic writing (for "Dubai") on a wall.

Similarly, we sought marketing images for the films identified as among the most profitable each year, selecting from those identified as having a character, setting, or plot featuring the Middle East. Action-adventure films promoted marketing images that featured the heroes and their conquests, such as in *Black Hawk Down*,

X-Men: Days of Future Past, *GI Joe*, *Iron Man 3*, *Mission Impossible: Ghost Protocol*, *Skyfall*, *Taken*, and *the Bourne Ultimatum*, although these marketing images did not consistently include landscapes or other visual signifiers. In contrast, films celebrating mythical and historical figures did include Middle Eastern references in their marketing images, such as pharaohs, pyramids, and Islamic art in *Night at the Museum*, *Lara Croft Tomb Raider*, and *Prince of Persia*.

While popular culture may accentuate the mythical when referencing Egypt, conflict becomes more central in images associated with action-adventure films and games. Given that news media focus on contemporary events, these constructions of the region highlight conflict and are resonant with images of fighting and heroism in public culture marketing. Development and military intervention carry through these themes of conquest and rescue, positioning the superiority of the United States with attempts to justify action and investment.

Prevalent mapping then positions agency and superiority within the United States by using stereotyped desert landscapes and conflict-ridden scenes. These visual references serve to justify development aid that is meant to generate goodwill and to support technologies and youth, which represent modernity and rationality. Israel appears as a partner in development and policy, as well as a large recipient of US investment, whereas Egypt attracts development resources but is more known in US articulations through the myths and mysteries associated with its past. Contemporary maps assert arenas for conflict and conquest, either directly or as a passive background for global theater. These representations mostly lack a construction of partnership and instead engage in objectification. Next, I consider how certain maps tend to prevail and endure.

Enduring Maps over Time

In this section, I consider more closely how dominant mapping endures over time and to what extent shifts in historical circumstances might engender adjustments in constructions of the region and visual references. Although the broad mission of development remains consistent over time, the strategic visions toward particular issues and regions vary with historical circumstances and domestic politics. First, I summarize key features in the US–Middle East relationship in the past twenty-five years.

US Intervention in the Middle East

In this section, I offer a concise and abbreviated recent history of US intervention in the Middle East (see Figure 2 for a timeline). Because I am focusing on a particular time period, this summary is quite brief, without the complexity and depth of other significant texts on the subject (Chalcraft, 2016; Cole, 2015). Although official US engagement with the region encapsulates complex and varying approaches, I highlight some of the central features of foreign aid and military intervention over the last quarter century in order to contrast shifts in mapping over time, relevant to this research project.

Scholars reviewing the histories of these geopolitical dynamics within the Middle East suggest that power began to shift away from British imperialism after World War II as the United States became more concerned with its role as a global leader and with its interest in oil (Doran, 2019), both factors becoming increasingly relevant after the Vietnam War (Indyk, 2019). Later, with the end of Cold War politics and an accentuated concern with terrorism, the role of

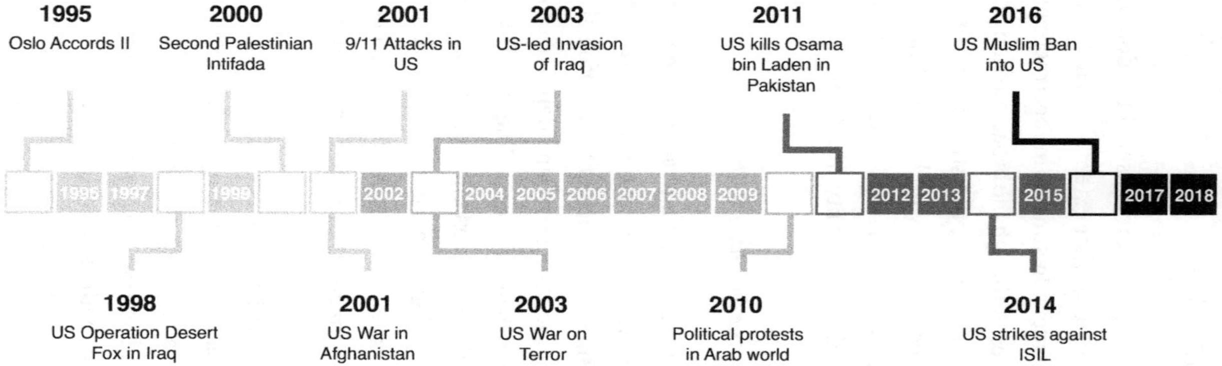

FIGURE 2. Recent historical timeline United States / Middle East. Graphic by Alexandra Chavez.

the United States became even more pronounced in regional politics, evidenced in extensive and costly military operations, economic integration, and cultural connections (Fleck & Kilby, 2010; Juneau, 2014). Current attention to US foreign policy recognizes the significance of shifting away from Cold War politics toward what some more recently, since 2016, would refer to as a break with historical policies and international law, lacking clarity and vision (Telhami, 2019).

How have historical conditions shifted between the United States and the region in the last quarter century? To characterize this period, I consider the mid-1990s leading up to 9/11 2001; 2002–2010, with 2011 and the following years marking the emergence of substantial political protests in the region as well as the rise of ISIL, until 2016, marking the election of Donald Trump as president of the United States. Although the official US record of military intervention does not encompass all activity in relation to conflict and competition, the congressional records of official US armed services actions across the world do offer a basis for considering key public events as recorded in an official record (Torreon, 2017).

In the five years just prior to 9/11, the United States initiated military operations in Afghanistan, Iraq, and Yemen, bombing other areas in the region as well, and imposed sanctions on Iraq and on foreign companies investing in Iran and Libya (1996). Operation Desert Strike, a missile attack against Iraq, also launched in 1996, with subsequent military campaigns in 1998 known as Operation Desert Fox. While these areas became direct sites for U.S. intervention, Palestinian communities initiated an intifada in the year prior to 9/11, following frustrations over diplomatic negotiations in Oslo in 1993. Political dialogue was also challenged with the assassination of Israeli prime minister Yitzhak Rabin by Israeli extremists in 1995, and then failed diplomacy attempts in 2000 by US president Bill Clinton (Doran, 2019; Makdisi, 2016). Throughout these negotiations and military strikes, US foreign policy was guided by "support for Israel" (Telhami, 2019), the "protection of vital petroleum supplies," and the "fight against international terrorism" (Sharp, 2009).

Following devastating violence in 2001, the United States intensified military interventions in Iraq and Afghanistan, and over time in other areas such as Pakistan and Yemen. The year 2003 represents a critical moment, with the intensification of US intervention in Iraq, marked with official pronouncements by President Bush and investments in military and development programs. This was also a time when the United States was pursuing a "freedom agenda" intended to promote democratic governance and free markets (Yahya, 2019).

US foreign aid to the region grew dramatically after World War II, and again in its post-9/11 phase to build programs designed to promote democracy and to stimulate "socio-economic reform in order to undercut the forces of radicalism in some Arab countries" (Sharp, 2009).

Relevant to our consideration of public images, in 2003 the US government issued the "Dover Ban," prohibiting media from projecting images and videos of dead American soldiers, which was not lifted until 2009 (Purnell, 2018). Various negotiations attempting peace plans, in 2003 (including the Geneva Initiative), 2007 (the Annapolis Conference), 2010 (in Washington, D.C.), and others over time have failed. Although to a lesser extent than in Iraq and Afghanistan, the US armed services also are recorded as directly intervening in Lebanon in 2006, Libya in 2011–12, Yemen in 2012, and Jordan in 2013 (Torreon, 2017). In addition to military projects, in 2006 the United States led the UN Security Council in approving sanctions against Iran and worked in collaboration with Israel against Iran in subsequent years (2008 and 2010).

Following continuing and failing negotiations with Israeli authorities through dominant global public agencies, such as the European Union and the United Nations (2003 "roadmap," with United States and Russia as well), Palestinians in Gaza elected Hamas leadership (2006), while those in the West Bank sustained their PLO governance. During this time (2005) Lebanese prime minister Rafiq Hariri was assassinated in a car bombing, inspiring public protests against Syrian military control, known as the Cedar Revolution (Chalcraft, 2016).

As the threats from al-Qaida and the Taliban began to be eclipsed by that of the Islamic State of Iraq and the Levant (variously known as ISIL, ISIS, or Daesh), US armed services expanded their territorial claims to include Syria, Turkey, Egypt, Jordan, and Kuwait. Air strikes against Daesh began in 2014, intensifying in 2015 and continuing through the period of this study. Through direct and indirect support, the United States has focused on combat from the air and training others, such as groups in Syria, to fight on the ground; since 2017, there has been sustained and direct US military intervention in Syria, Iraq, and Afghanistan (Torreon, 2017). The George W. Bush presidency was characterized as pursuing more direct and more unilateral military action in the region in contrast to President Obama's leadership, which has been described as less interventionist, relying instead on soft power and indirect support (Krieg, 2016).

While the threat of Daesh has been used to justify US military intervention, the celebration of Arab youth in popular protests since 2011 has inspired public support (Doran, 2019). These local challenges have had regional and global significance, relevant not only to national aspirations but to nonstate actors, such as Houthis, Kurds, and Daesh as well (Malley, 2019). The US media have enthusiastically supported the various popular protests occurring across the northern African region, with dominant frames applauding the youth and social media featured in these stories (Ghobrial & Wilkins, 2015; Wilkins, 2012).

Contrasted with the relative public support in the United States for these seemingly youthful rebellions, similar political protests in Iran have had less of a sympathetic recognition and appreciation in public discourse. Instead, Iran has been portrayed as an existential threat in dominant US discourse since 1979 (Chomsky, 2016), given that "Iran fits neatly into a well-defined American idea of what a serious threat should look like" (Benjamin & Simon, 2019, p. 60).

In the years following these protests in the Arab region, other than Tunisia most communities experienced worsening conditions in terms of economic growth and poverty, media freedoms, food security, and other development indicators (Yahya, 2019). As conditions declined, a new culture of protest has strengthened movements in Algerian and Sudanese communities more recently, following those in Iraq, Jordan, Lebanon, Morocco, and others revived from earlier years (Yahya, 2019). Lynch (2007) and others recognized an emerging public sphere with the emergence of Al Jazeera and other interactive digital communication technologies leading up to the 2010 protests in the region.

Although foreign policy rhetoric may have shifted to the Asian region with the advent of Obama's administration, political protests in the Arab region ("Arab Spring") and the rise of Daesh attracted US media attention, which strengthened the importance of the Middle East as a "US priority" (Krieg, 2016, p. 106). Krieg

(2016) sees this era as one in which the United States engages in "surrogate warfare," relying more heavily on allies and partners to carry out direct combat operations, as well as non-state actors (such as the Free Syrian Army) and technologies (such as drones), thereby intervening less publicly and directly, given US public opposition to military involvement.

Recent reviews of US foreign policy toward the Middle East (*Foreign Affairs* Special Issue, 2019) chronicle a turn toward rashly conceived and poorly executed directives and practices since the election of Donald Trump. Having transcended the British Empire as a dominant actor in the twentieth century, US power within the region has become increasingly challenged by Russian and Chinese activities. President Trump's unabashed allegiances to Israel, and to Saudi Arabia—despite the finding of that government's guilt in the murder of prominent US-based journalist Jamal Khashoggi (Indyk, 2019; Malley, 2019)—as well as other global actions, signal the prioritizing of global capitalism against interest in global moral leadership.

Military action has overshadowed more diplomatic approaches to political engagement, alongside intensive and significant economic contributions through public and private channels. In the next section, I focus on a portion of this broader set of capital investment, targeting official development assistance given its public and official relevance.

U.S. Investment in the Middle East

Recognizing that investments take on many forms and contribute through a variety of public and private channels, here I concentrate on official development assistance between the United States and

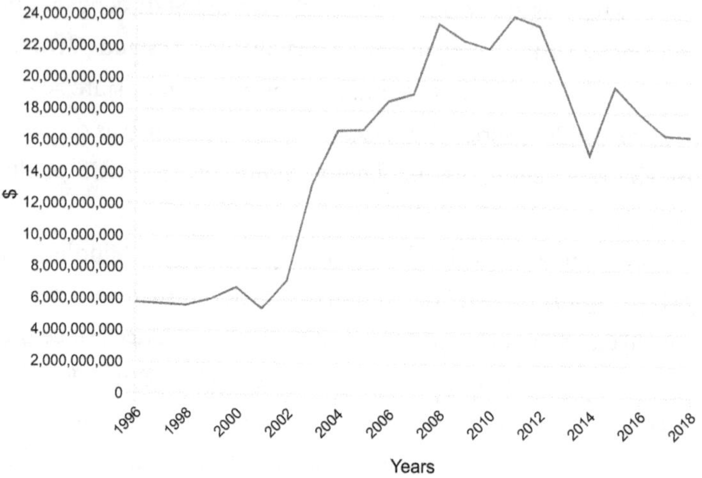

FIGURE 3. US foreign aid to the Middle East

countries that it designates as in the Middle East (see Figure 3). For many years US aid to Israel represented the highest allocation to any one country in the region. Recently its typical allocation of $3 billion per year was surpassed by expenditures in Iraq ($3.4 billion) and in Afghanistan ($4.9 billion). The US allocation to Israel spiked in 2000 and 2003, the latter year also marking a dramatic increase in aid to Jordan at roughly $2 billion, though typically not higher than $1.5 billion. While the amount accorded to direct bilateral aid has fluctuated over time, Jordan has been a leading recipient of US aid since the 1990s (Sharp, 2009), rising steadily since 2008. US aid to the West Bank and Gaza gradually increased from rather small amounts through 2008, with the highest allocations of about $1 billion in 2009–10 and 2013, then was reduced steadily over time to less than $400 million. For many years Egypt had been high on the recipient list of US aid, though this amount began to decline beginning in 2010, with annual allocations now typically under $1.5 billion.

At much lower amounts (each under $100 million), allocations to Algeria have been steadily rising since 2005, with Morocco spiking in 2008, and Libya attracting more assistance in 2011, sustaining allocations at slightly reduced rates in 2012 but still receiving more aid than prior to 2011. Aid to Lebanon rose in 2006, increasing through 2015 and then fell slightly, more recently disbursing about $300–$400 million. US aid to Syria did not come into play until 2012, with much higher amounts allocated since 2013 (about $600–$700 million); similarly, Tunisia started receiving more substantial amounts since 2011 (about $130 million), with a peak in 2012.

Given their stark contrast in wealth compared to North Africa and the Levant, countries in the Gulf have been the targets of development less often than others in the region. Between 2005 and 2007, Kuwait was the recipient of higher amounts of aid, fluctuating over time, and more recently saw an increase in 2017 (about $4 million). In proximity to Kuwait, Bahrain received less funding in comparison, though it had much higher aid allocations committed in 1996 and again in 2003, the latter being the same year Oman received its highest allocation.

While Iran does not regularly receive US aid, its highest allocation was in 2004, followed by 2007. This was the same year (2007) that included an increase to the UAE, with much lower but sustained funding from 2011. Including Qatar in US assistance did not begin in any substantial sense until 2005, peaking in 2009, with almost no aid since 2011. Saudi Arabia also peaked in its allocation of US aid in 2006 and 2011–12, with some aid earlier in 1996–98 and later sustained contributions since 2002. US aid to Yemen did not start to increase until 2010, with its highest allocations in 2013 and then 2017.

Over time there have been considerable shifts in allocations to countries in the region. Iraq received substantial funding, along with military intervention, initiated through the U.S. invasion in March 2003, with no funding prior to that in the preceding decade. In concert with military intervention, US aid to Afghanistan began to rise from 2003 until peaking in 2011, with gradually decreasing amounts since then but still relatively higher than that of many other recipients (remaining at over $4 billion).

Corresponding with the time periods considered in the brief historical summary above, in the few years preceding 9/11, Israel and Egypt were the largest recipients of US foreign assistance. Over 2000–2009, U.S. investment also included more attention to Iraq, Jordan, and Afghanistan, the latter accruing proportionately more over time, with more recent increases to Syria, Yemen, the West Bank, and Gaza. While the focus of this foreign assistance is of interest, even more is the dramatic increase in US aid since post-9/11 and peaking in 2010, approximately around the time of public protests in the region.

US News of the Middle East

Next I consider how attention to the Middle East as a region has changed (see Figure 4). Documenting the pattern of explicit attention to the "Middle East" over time, these television news broadcasts peaked in their coverage in 2002 (n = 881 stories), with a gradual buildup beginning in 2000, after reaching a low in 1999 from a downward slope in attention since 1996. Following a period of more attention from 2000 to 2003, the frequency of recognition

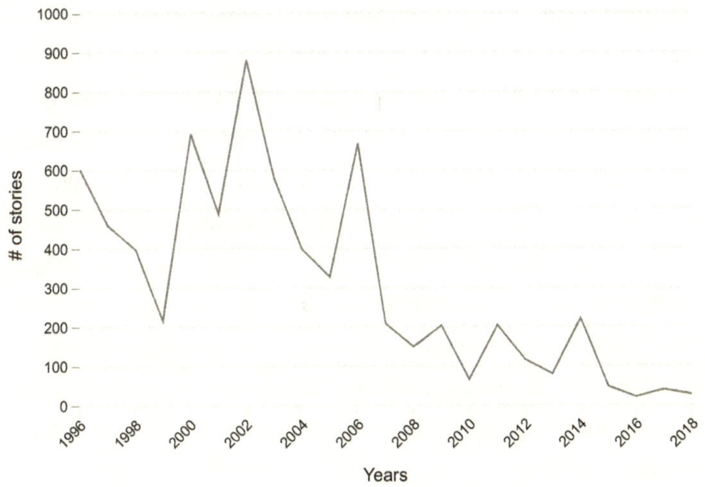

FIGURE 4. US TV broadcast news of the Middle East. Vanderbilt archives: evening news 1996–2018 from ABC, CBS, CNN, NBC

of the region was cut in half, until 2006 ($n = 668$), followed by a steep and sustained decline other than a brief peak in 2014. With the average number of news items at 317 and a median of 211 overall, clearly the peak years include 1996, 2000–2003, and 2006. The increase in coverage each of these years is proportionate to the trends in the central subjects of these news stories, following the proportion of stories relevant to US involvement in political stories as well as coverage of violence.

These trends in visibility over time directly relate to attention given to politics and violence (not mutually exclusive), while stories on economic and cultural issues in the region remain consistently low over time. Coverage of violence was most acute in 2001–2 and 2006, explained in part through intensified attention to conflict in Palestinian and Israeli communities, most frequently documented in 1996, 2001–3, and 2006, these also being the peak years of coverage in TV news overall. The proportion of stories devoted to coverage of violence exceeded half of all coverage in the years 1997–98, 2001–3, 2006–7, 2009, and 2012–15, particularly important in the more recent years given that overall news coverage had been dramatically reduced from its most recent peak in 2006.

Television news coverage of the Middle East centers largely around increased military intervention 2001–3 and again in 2006, with heightened attention to Israeli confrontations in Gaza and with Lebanon. Similarly, the post-9/11 years saw an increase in foreign assistance, though this trend continued through 2010 prior to a relative decline.

US Films Referencing the Middle East

To what extent did US films follow the pattern of news attention to the Middle East over time? Only 10 percent of the top twenty films over this more than two-decade period reference the "Middle East," averaging about two per year (see Figure 5). Prior to 9/11, this sample of popular films referenced the Middle East consistently at about two per year, with this trend roughly consistent, noting four in 2009. The years 2012 ($n = 5$) and 2015 ($n = 6$) screened the most over this period, raising the mean level of attention to the region to three per year since 2010. These broad trends are supported by the finding that films referencing the region in a more central way have also increased over time.

This more recent proportion of attention to the region in popular film does not follow the trends in US news coverage, mostly devoted to the region in the immediate post-9/11 era. However, a boost in popular films referencing the region does appear more

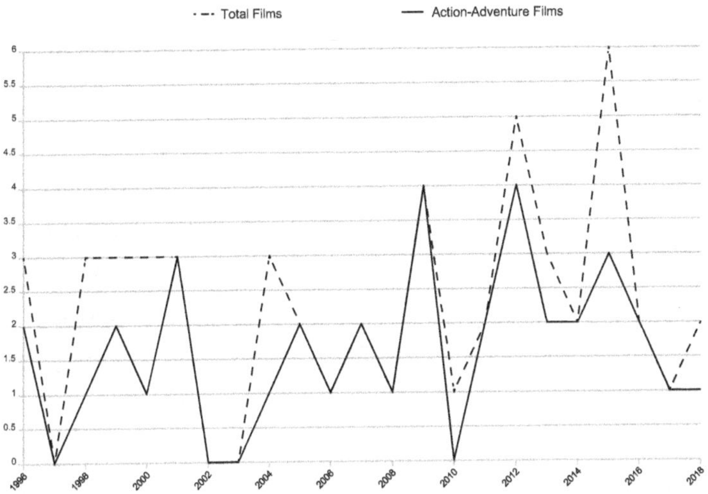

FIGURE 5. US films referencing the Middle East

closely aligned with proportional attention to violence within TV news, documented also in 2009, 2012, and in 2014–15.

Among the forty-nine films identified with a Middle East reference in the annual lists of the most popular films, most fall within an action-adventure genre (75%), followed by science fiction and fantasy (25%) and children's programming (15%; these are not mutually exclusive categories). Similar to the patterns described above, action-adventure featured most frequently in 2001, 2009, 2012, and 2015, related to years in which TV news broadcasts were more likely to focus on violence than other issues. Overall though, the television news focus on the Middle East has been declining, while proportional attention in popular film has been gradually rising along with financial allocations to foreign assistance.

While these trends capture frequency of attention, not all recognition is constructive. Action-adventure dominates these films, particularly after 9/11, in 2000–2001, 2005–9, 2011–12, and 2015. Moreover, films produced in more recent years are much more likely to be set in contemporary and not historical time periods.

The events of 9/11 did inspire more US investment in the region, as well as more news attention initially. Following a dramatic initial increase in frequency of news stories on the region, attention began to decline, rising again 2006–2007 before falling again. While US funding remained higher than in pre-9/11 times, attention to the region gradually rose in popular films. Next, I consider how these maps work across agencies and genres.

Mapping the Middle East

Recognizing that the boundaries demarcating the circumference of the region referred to as the "Middle East" are as complex, porous, and shifting as are its internal borders, official U.S. agencies' definitions of the region, through their explicit conceptualizations, project implementations, and financial investments, demonstrate diverse maps that assert the interests of the state. At the heart of each of these maps we see various configurations of proximate Arab nations, typically including those in the Levant and the Gulf. Arab nations in the Levant are highlighted as "modern," and "entrepreneurial" in foreign assistance descriptions, while those in the Gulf are recognized as sites of economic wealth, as well as sites for conflict. Arab countries across northern Africa have also become integrated into these maps, though they may also be included in other configurations of the African region. When considered part of the "Middle East," they leverage official attention as sites for development, diplomacy, and potential movements for democracy.

The areas of the Middle East that do not fit conceptual mapping that privileges Arab communities include Iran, Israel, and Turkey, whose languages and cultures tend to be included in US universities that offer educational degrees and programs attributed to this region. These three countries, along with increasing attention to Afghanistan in this conceptual mapping, are part of what official US resources now call a "New Middle East," notable for connecting military intervention and political conflict with proximate nations previously constituting a "traditional" Middle East. Referencing Turkey allows some of the official US work to extend toward central Asia as well, at times included in this categorization, disregarding Turkey's alliances with its European neighbors.

Although US agencies work across a variety of countries, from military impositions to development programs, U.S. television news concentrates on violence mostly in connection with Israeli, Palestinian, and Iraqi contexts. Very little attention was paid to cultural or even economic concerns, eclipsed by the almost exclusive focus on politics and problems. The general tenor of this coverage was more negative, angry, and simplistic than other news coverage in general, as will be described in the next chapter. Concentration on conflict in news stories resonates with that of popular US films, given that the mapping is asserted through action-adventure films.

Visual images of the Middle East offer portrayals of entrepreneurial women and aspiring youth through photographs accompanying USAID literature, whereas marketing images of popular films and video games emphasize the military and combative prowess of men fighting in locations such as Iraq, Afghanistan, Iran, and Istanbul. These images support mapping that asserts development needs designed to aid women and children, who are projected as needing help, thus justifying foreign aid, as well as military intervention, and asserting the power and necessity of heroic engagement. While these themes contribute to the assertion of constructed maps, their narrative function will be explored in more depth in the following chapter.

While the visual images used in marketing development and popular culture resonated with development and military intervention, attention to Egypt was more likely to assert a map of a mythical site, distant in historical time and space, though still home to adventure and conquest. These maps use signifiers such as pyramids in deserts, mummies in tombs, and women in veils and head coverings to situate the image in the "Middle East." In contrast to other communities gaining prominence in these maps through their potential for violence or their despair, Egypt's role in popular culture tends to rely on a mapping that is more obscure and less connected to contemporary events. When Egypt does feature in television news, relative to coverage of other Middle East events this country tends to explicate the role of US presidents or other national officials (particularly Secretary of State Condoleezza Rice (2005–2009). The importance of Egypt to the United States is demonstrated in its history as a top recipient of foreign assistance in the region for years before a steady decline in funding since 2010.

These maps make visible the areas that fit conceptualizations of communities that require rescue, through development assistance, military intervention, or masculine heroics. Although there are political alliances and collaborations between the United States and many of these countries, there is much less attention given to existing or potential partnerships. Also less visible are the internal dynamics within and across cultural communities, or the areas of cultural pride and social achievements.

The mediated maps of the Middle East constructed in the United States assert configurations of territories that serve the needs of state political and economic interests through the work of official agencies, the reporting of news, and the stories in popular culture. The marketing images used to support this work offer resonant frameworks in support of these constructions. Despite the documented concerns with not only the lack of consensus of what defines this as a region, but also the particular hubris guiding this articulation, this mapping of the Middle East endures. In the next chapter I consider in more depth the narratives engaged that are meant to describe the Middle East.

3 *Narrating the Middle East*

Narration builds on an articulation of mapping: situating story and sequence given an asserted place and constructed space. In this chapter, I build connections across dominant themes in mediated narratives and investigate the prominence of violence and conflict as foundational to narratives of despair, requiring a rescue (whether through fictional heroes, official development, or military intervention); narratives of conquest, building on assumptions of blank slates and weak states that are meant to justify empire; and narratives of magical kingdoms, devoid of historical context or of contemporary politics.

This study supports earlier work demonstrating the importance of action adventure to US mediations of the Middle East. When US popular culture does integrate characters, landscapes, or issues from the Middle East, it is much more likely to do so through action-adventure than other genres, such as comedy or romantic drama (Alsultany, 2012, 2016; McAlister, 2005; McKee, 1997; Neale, 2004; Shaheen, 2001; Wilkins, 2009). Action-adventure has been critiqued for relying on an oversimplification of complex events and characters, typically asserting a lone masculine hero (though female heroes are gaining in visibility) who vanquishes evil, personified through Muslim, Arab male villains (Dittmer, 2005; Shaheen, 2001; Wilkins & Downing, 2002). McAlister (2005) notes that the "hostage rescue quickly became a staple of American action movies" (p. 224), at the time of her publication referencing *Star Wars* (1977); *Alien* (1979); *Raiders of the Lost Ark* (1981), as well as *Die Hard* (1988). Analyses of popular film in this study confirm the prominence of action-adventure when referencing the Middle East. These findings fit the framework posited in terms of focus on rescue and conquest in action-adventure and on the mythical and mystical in other genres.

The privileging of action-adventure as a genre in popular culture supports dominant themes of rescue and conquest, which resonate with news and development discourse. Across sources, these rescue narratives determine how problems are explained, and how heroic solutions are justified, in gendered frameworks that accentuate distinctions across cultural and national communities. Situating violence as a product of male "Middle Eastern" terrorists harming vulnerable women, then, assigns Northern and Western men value through an "action rescue" narrative. Moreover, technologies become part of the armor and weapons of heroes.

Related to rescue is the mission of conquest, in which those with power are considered to be justified in acquiring land, artifacts, or civilizations, from the standpoint of their projected expertise and goodwill. This mission is also based on an assumption that indigenous agents lack ability or interest in such efforts as preserving art, extracting oil, excavating tombs, or implementing development programs. The assumption also performs the task of not identifying US reliance on oil produced in other countries. Thus, projecting the Middle East as an empty slate becomes foundational to an "empire adventure" narrative.

These empire adventure narratives, rooted in a broader action-adventure framework, also tend to be positioned within magical circumstances with supernatural creatures. This contributes toward a broader category of films situated within a "magical kingdom" narrative. This framework accentuates the fantastical and supernatural and avoids historical context and specific political interests, serving to distance these cultural references from contemporary politics and concerns. Rooted in historical contexts are another set of films, though few, that situate stories in the region and project varying degrees of authenticity.

These narratives are explored across popular culture, news, and development to characterize the prevalence of certain themes, as well as their endurance over time. While most of the exploration of popular culture focuses on film, to supplement analyses video games and television shows are also included. It is not the effects of a single text that are of concern, but rather of the accumulation of images dehumanizing and depoliticizing Arab and Muslim cultures.

Analyses of narratives consider both manifest dimensions of content as well as latent implications in texts. As a form of discourse, narratives are explored as sequences of events with particular emphases in story structures. The themes proposed as guiding US media, whether fictional or informational, are not meant as mutually exclusive categories, but rather as articulations of different emphases. The dominant narratives stem from action-adventure frameworks, described here in terms of their concentration on rescue as central to the suspenseful sequence of events, as well as on conquest as critical to the culmination of plots featuring adventure.

Action Rescue Narrative

Narratives relying on rescue as an appropriate intervention build on establishing serious devastation from violent events, which justify strong and assertive action. The assumption that violence is a central part of life in the region is supported by the dominance of this theme in US news coverage.

US News

Violence begets crises, necessitating active rescue missions. Reviewing US television news transcripts over time, violence (58%) and conflict clearly register often in the framing of stories of the Middle East, with political stories (73%) also featuring confrontation. Less prominent are potentially constructive political collaborations and cultural connections or even economic disparities in relation to global capital. These themes fit the documented tenor of US news on global issues and on other regions more broadly. What makes coverage of this particular region stand out is its emphasis on violence and conflict, whether internal, cross-national, or involving the US military. For example, coverage describes Iraq's alleged "weapons of mass destruction" and US strikes and attacks, Palestinian "terrorists" and Israeli "troops" and "attacks," and Yemeni and Syrian "unrest." It is important to note that these findings result from a sample of mainstream television news, whereas other sources might exhibit other frames, such as "magical kingdoms" in relation to business coverage.

As referenced in the previous chapter, words associated with violence are frequently used explicitly in this coverage. Next,

I consider how the psychometric properties of these news descriptions fare in terms of their orientations in contrast with general news as documented by the authors of the Linguistic Inquiry and Word Count (LIWC) software system (Pennebaker, Boyd, Jordan, & Blackburn, 2015). Their assessment includes only articles published in the *New York Times* January through July 2014, whereas the sample I used consists of television news summaries from 1996 through 2018. Recognizing the differences in timing and source, the comparison depicted in Table 2 offers a rough contrast in how news coverage of the Middle East specifically differs from news more generally.

Using this LIWC processing to assign specific words to predetermined psychometric properties, some clear differences arise. LIWC positions words in an existing dictionary, aligning them within various references determined through previously conducted, well-documented psychology research. News of the Middle East is considerably less positive (1.27 compared with 2.32) and much more negative than news in general (2.76 compared with 1.45), as well as much more likely to use words associated with anger (1.36 compared with .47) and anxiety (.57 compared with .25). Words connotating religious affiliations are also more likely to be used in discussions of the Middle East (1.02) than in general news (.25). It is also worth noting that the cognitive level of the vocabulary used is much more simplistic (3.80) than that of other news (7.52), though this may also be a function of these samples consisting of television news in the case of the former and *New York Times* print news in the latter.

US news and popular films offer strikingly similar narratives, despite different industrial and societal expectations. Beydoun (2018) characterizes similarities between heroic pursuits against

TABLE 2. Psychometric Properties of Middle East News in Contrast to General News

	Middle East	News in General
Positive emotions	1.27	2.32
Negative emotions	2.76	1.45
Anxious emotions	.57	.25
Anger emotions	1.36	.47
Cognitive level	3.80	7.52
Religious reference	1.02	.25
Word count for abstracts	39,430	26,007,632

villainous exploits in US news as similar to the Orientalist binaries in *American Sniper* (2015), *True Lies* (1994), *Executive Decision* (1996), and other films, centering terrorism within the domain of Islam. Other analyses of US news coverage of Palestinian issues illustrate a remarkable similarity to the narrative of the film *The Siege* (Noakes & Wilkins, 2002; Wilkins & Downing, 2002). Next, the analyses consider the role of this narrative in mediated popular culture.

US Popular Culture

Films referencing the Middle East rely on action-rescue narratives that build on a foundation of violent conflict central to the story. The sample of films ($n = 49$) is composed of those designated as having a reference to the Middle East among the top twenty grossing films each year from 1995 to 2018. Examples from the list of thirty-one action-adventure films (63%) include *The English Patient* (1996), *Black Hawk Down* (2001), *Taken* (2009; 2012), and *American Sniper* (2014; see Figure 6). This is similar to the percentage of

TABLE 3. Popular Films Referencing the Middle East

Year	Title	Coding	Narrative
1995	None		
1996	*The Rock*	Minor plot	Action Rescue
	The English Patient	Minor character/ Major setting	Action Rescue
	Broken Arrow	Minor plot	Action Rescue
1997	None		
1998	*The Waterboy*	Minor plot	Comedy
	Enemy of the State	Minor plot	Action Rescue
	The Prince of Egypt	Major character/ setting/plot	Magical Kingdom
1999	*Austin Powers: The Spy Who Shagged Me*	Minor setting	Comedy/Action Rescue
	The Matrix	Minor setting	Action Rescue/ Magical Kingdom
	The Mummy	Major character/ plot/setting	Empire Adventure/ Magical Kingdom
	The World Is Not Enough	Minor plot/ major setting	Action Rescue
2000	*Gladiator*	Minor setting/ Minor character	Historical Drama
2001	*The Mummy Returns*	Major character/ plot/ setting	Empire Adventure/ Magical Kingdom
	Lara Croft: Tomb Raider	Minor setting	Empire Adventure/ Magical Kingdom
	Black Hawk Down	Minor character	Action Rescue
2002	None		
2003	None		
2004	*The Passion of the Christ*	Major setting/ characters	Historical Drama
	National Treasure	Minor plot	Empire Adventure
	Fahrenheit 9/11	Minor plot	Documentary

Year	Title	Coding	Narrative
2005	*Batman Begins*	Major character	Action Rescue/ Magical Kingdom
	Flightplan	Minor characters	Action Rescue
2006	*Night at the Museum*	Major character	Empire Adventure/ Magical Kingdom
2007	*The Bourne Ultimatum*	Minor setting	Action Rescue
	300	Minor setting/ characters	Historical Drama
2008	*Iron Man*	Minor setting/ characters	Action Rescue
2009	*Transformers: Revenge of the Fallen*	Minor setting	Action Rescue/ Magical Kingdom
	Night at the Museum: Battle of the Smithsonian	Major character	Empire Adventure/ Magical Kingdom
	G.I. Joe: The Rise of Cobra	Major setting	Action Rescue
	Taken	Major character	Action Rescue
2010	*Despicable Me*	Minor setting	Action Rescue/ Magical Kingdom
2011	*Transformers: Dark of the Moon*	Minor setting/ characters	Action Rescue/ Magical Kingdom
	Mission: Impossible - Ghost Protocol	Major setting	Action Rescue
2012	*The Dark Knight Rises*	Major character	Action Rescue
	Skyfall	Minor setting	Action Rescue
	The Twilight Saga: Breaking Dawn Part 2	Minor characters	Action Rescue/ Magical Kingdom
	Taken 2	Major setting	Action Rescue
2013	*Iron Man 3*	Minor setting	Action Rescue
	World War Z	Major setting/ characters	Action Rescue/ Magical Kingdom

(*continued*)

TABLE 3. *(continued)*

Year	Title	Coding	Narrative
2014	*American Sniper*	Major setting/ characters	Action Rescue
	X-Men: Days of Future Past	Minor setting	Action Rescue/ Magical Kingdom
2015	*Star Wars: The Force Awaken*	Minor setting	Action Rescue/ Magical Kingdom
	Fast and Furious 7	Minor setting	Empire Adventure
	Minions	Minor setting	Comedy/ Magical Kingdom
	The Martian	Minor setting	Empire Adventure
	Spectre	Minor setting	Action Rescue
	Mission: Impossible – Rogue Nation	Major setting	Action Rescue
2016	*Suicide Squad*	Minor setting	Action Rescue/ Magical Kingdom
	X-Men: Apocalypse	Major setting/ characters	Action Rescue/ Magical Kingdom
2017	*Wonder Woman*	Minor setting/ character	Action Rescue/ Magical Kingdom
2018	*Bohemian Rhapsody*	Major character/ Minor reference	Drama
	Mission Impossible: Fallout	Major setting	Action Rescue

news coverage of conflict described above. Given the dominance of conflict in these plots, it is worth noting that when the plot is directly related to the Middle East in settings or major characters, it tends to build on a concern or problem that is caused by a character from this region (90%), though rarely does such a character solve that problem. Instead, the heroes of these narratives are positioned as North American or European (97%).

FIGURE 6. *American Sniper* (2014)

In addition to the analysis above considering each film as a unit of analysis, central characters were also considered (n = 202 characters) and designated as hero, victim, or villain, if clearly described as such, and in terms of appearance or other identifying features. Among those identified as heroes, most (83%) appeared lighter in skin tone and were identified as part of the global North, with few (12%) as darker in skin tone and identified with the global South. Conforming to established patterns in previous scholarship, villains and victims were more likely to be identified with the global South and global South characters were more likely to be registered in coding as secondary (96%) than primary characters (14%). Combining analysis of primary and secondary characters from the Middle East, most were ascribed villain status rather than hero. The few heroes connected with the Middle East tend to be included in mythical narratives, such as the Scorpion King in *Mummy Returns*, or Moses and Jesus in biblical films. Examples of villains include men from Iraq, such as those featured in *American Sniper*, as well as groups of unnamed men from Afghanistan or Persia, as in *Iron Man* or *300*. In *Taken*, groups of Arab men appear to be appreciating the trafficking of women by Albanian gangs, thwarted by a lone white male, formerly affiliated with the CIA, whose daughter has been captured. When this protagonist references villains, he asserts that they are "from the East" and are, therefore, "dangerous."

To explore the resonance of these themes in popular culture more broadly, I consider how popular films referencing the Middle East relate to popular fictional television series and video games. These analyses focus on the decade 2005–2014. Over this ten-year period, among the two hundred relevant films, we identified twenty relevant to this study, or 10 percent of this broader population of top-grossing films.

While the genres identified across these top two hundred films were diverse, those exhibiting any connection to Arab, Israeli, Iranian, or Turkish communities were decidedly focused on action-adventure or dramatic thriller genres. Reviewing a similar list of the top twenty television shows broadcast in the United States from 2005 to 2014 (based on statistics published by the *Hollywood Reporter*), we witness a similar trend to that of popular film, in that not quite 10 percent (17/200 possible top-twenty shows over the ten-year period observed) address the Middle East in setting, plot, or character; and among those that do, most are dramas that involve solving mysteries or crimes (such as *Lost*, *CSI*, *NCIS*, *Scandal*, and *Blacklist*) or build on fantasies (*Once Upon a Time*); the latter is relevant to my subsequent discussion of the "magical kingdom" narrative.

Accentuating the cultural lens of fictional television and film, video games are even more likely to rely on simplistic narratives that position Western heroes against Muslim and Arab villains (Šisler, 2008). Some of the games produced in this industry explicitly situate play within a Middle Eastern setting or employ characters of clear Middle Eastern origin. Reviewing the top five best-selling games between 2005 and 2014 (VGCharz.com, 2015), the most relevant series was *Call of Duty*, in various manifestations (such as *Black Ops*, *Ghosts*, *Advanced Warfare*) and across platforms (mostly x360 and some ps3). Other top-selling video games not visualizing the Middle East include titles such as *Nintendo*, *Mario*, *Wii Sports*, *Grand Theft Auto*, and *Pokémon*. Other games relying on US military forces acting heroically in the face of terrorists identified with Middle East communities such as those in Iraq, Iran, or Dubai include *Army of Two* (2008), *Battlefield 3* (2011), *Spec Ops: The Line* (2012), *Splinter Cell: Blacklist* (2013), with *Call of Duty 4* (2007) involving UK soldiers. The few games that reference Middle Eastern characters in positive as well as negative roles clearly distinguish between them through the visuals of shading skin and clothing in lighter versus darker tones, a trend repeated in other games in which terrorists are delineated from American and British soldiers and executives acting as heroes. This trend resonates with themes explained by Naber (2014) relating whiteness to empire.

Military action guides narratives in films as well as video games, relying on tropes used in news coverage of the Gulf War, which itself has been likened to visual sequences in video games (McAlister, 2005). Narratives in news stories, films, and games assert the United States as dominant against racialized and foreign others in stories of conflict and conquest. Alsultany (2012) chronicles the emergence of multicultural teams of heroes, embodying, for example in *The Siege* (1998), a "distinctly liberal narrative of race and foreign policy" (p. 259); this film relies on a familiar trope that distinguishes "good" Arab citizens" from those who are terrorists.

From the evil Ra's and Talia al Ghul fighting *Batman*, to the evil ancient Pharaoh cursing the innocence of the American museum, terrorists with consistently darker skin tones challenge more lightly shaded men, such as ancient Persians fighting Greeks in *300* (2007); terrorists threatening *Iron Man* (2013), and Iraqi enemies shooting at the *American Sniper* (2014). The heroes of these narratives, consistently, are white straight men, mostly American, but if not, then Western European.

Apart from these emphases on action and violence, the rescue narrative structures particular roles for heroes, victims, and villains. The relationships across these roles follow predictable and repetitious patterns across media sources. While saving women becomes an overly pronounced theme used to justify intervention, American women are asserted as "free" in contrast. Both news coverage of Condoleezza Rice and film caricatures of Betty Mahmoody in *Not without My Daughter* (1991) illustrate the positive depictions of American women in juxtaposition with veiled women in Afghanistan or Iran (Alsultany, 2012; Cloud, 2004). But even American women may require rescue, as evidenced in the portrayal of American soldier Jessica Lynch in news coverage. The multicultural team of heroes described by Alsultany (2012) continues to surface, most recently with *Men in Black: International* (2019), featuring a smart, brave African American woman, publicly portrayed similarly to Condoleezza Rice as an individual not entangled by family and friends. Moreover, this character, Agent

M, explicitly expresses her desire to drive sophisticated cars, in contrast to news reports of women in Saudi Arabia, often erroneously generalized to the Gulf region, not being permitted to do so.

The gendered composition of vulnerability and venerability structures the narrative of rescue within popular culture. While the findings in this study clearly resonate with media scholarship more broadly, a particular bridge worth exploring connects action-rescue narratives in popular media with similar tropes in development discourse.

Key assumptions are that development aid is both necessary and effective, conflict and violence in the region require US intervention, and women and children need to be rescued. As a US-based "Hollywood" narrative, action heroes and US aid are expected to create happy endings, and through public relations strategies US government agents and agencies eagerly work to ensure that their acts are applauded and appreciated (Wilkins, 2018b). While the artificially happy endings (Ehrenreich, 2009) demarcate the narrative's conclusion, the justification for the conquest or conflict guiding the plot finds its foundation earlier in the narrative sequence.

US Development

A rescue narrative in which reasons justifying US intervention—whether through humanitarian, military, economic, or other programs—are difficult to resist needs to be understood across media landscapes. In this section I focus on development assistance narratives embedded in US official discussions of foreign aid to the region. I explore narrative themes that delineate regional development problems in relation to projected victims, their causes connected with archetypal villains, and the proposed solutions embodied in the acts of constructed heroes as part of an action rescue narrative.

The Middle East as an object of US development intervention figured in an early well-cited volume authored by Daniel Lerner (1958), explaining that "What America is . . . the modernizing Middle East seeks to become" (p. 79). US texts sustain their justification for development programs (Wilkins, 2004) by positioning the United States as a benign but necessary donor that rescues beleaguered Middle East victims from evil masculine (though in some caricatures emasculated) villains. These narratives highlight the role of individual agency in bringing about social change, privileging democratic and entrepreneurial themes.

The work of USAID represents a central set of strategies the United States government uses in its approach to allocating resources toward development in the Middle East. Within broader strategic goals established in the national interest, USAID promotes its role as a hero fighting to "end extreme poverty and to promote resilient, democratic societies while advancing our security and prosperity" (USAID, 2015k). To solve the problem of "extreme poverty," USAID intends to enable "inclusive, sustainable growth; promoting free, peaceful, and self-reliant societies with effective, legitimate governments; building human capital and creating social safety nets that reach the poorest and most vulnerable" (USAID, 2015k). This vulnerable community, then, serves as the victim in this narrative, a population that needs to be saved by "economic growth" and "accountable institutions" (USAID, 2015k). The portrayal of development recipients as victims also contributes to an assumption that addressing poverty helps prevent the actions of villains, namely, extremism.

Economic growth and prosperity dominate the central vision of USAID's goals in the Middle East. "Insufficient economic growth" and high "youth unemployment" are considered "major challenges" (USAID, 2015f). Education might be considered relevant to engaged citizenship, but here it is framed in terms of skills youth need to join the local workforce, particularly within the private sector. Skills for business, science, math, and "entrepreneurship" are favored, with the hope of strengthening "small- and medium-sized enterprises." Similar to focusing on women's participation in microenterprise schemes to allow them to build small businesses, this approach can be seen as infantilizing the recipients in its lack of attention to large-scale enterprise, the public sector, and significant leadership (USAID, 2015f; Wilkins, 2015).

Interest in modernization, particularly as a capitalist economic pursuit, is part of this rescue mission. Emphasizing the role of the private sector resonates with the work of Lerner, who privileges the entrepreneurial spirit of the grocer as emblematic of modernity and heroic within his context (Wilkins, 2004). Lerner's parable will be considered in more depth in the next section. What is missing from this vision of development, however, is the global context in which nations are encouraged to trade "freely" with the United States, even though they may go into debt doing so. Within the global sphere, a hierarchical positioning of countries enhances the abilities of some to the detriment of others. This global context loses visibility within USAID's programming for economic as well as political development.

While attention to democratic governance has been consistent in USAID's rhetoric for some time, recent political protests in the region, covered in television news, have allowed US discourse to promote itself as working in response to "citizens' demands," rather than imposing ideologies and structures. In concert with US development discourse more broadly, "accountability" is referenced as necessary for governments, and "participation in civil society" is encouraged. Support for "government-led reforms" is said to "foster more pluralistic, fair, responsive, and representative political leadership, and greater competition" (USAID, 2015k). Pluralist approaches to political participation and competitive potential underscores a liberal approach to political engagement, assuming individuals act with equal opportunities in fair circumstances.

More detailed discussions of civic and political engagement in 2015 explicitly raise interests in including diverse and vulnerable groups, specifically youth and women. Recent USAID programs support projects devoted to women in Egypt, Iraq, Jordan, and the West Bank/Gaza, the last of which also received specific funding devoted to youth. USAID documents from 2009 describe concerns with gender inequity, although these projects, like most development programs, are more likely to target women exclusively than address power imbalances across gender. Projects targeting women in the Middle East, when not channeling resources to women through their roles as mothers in population projects, tend to focus on encouraging women to run small private businesses by expanding their access to credit. Women are thus coded as victims of their cultural circumstances but are empowered to become heroic by subscribing to development project goals.

Recognizing that one of the particular conditions of this region is that it hosts "12 of the world's 15 most water-scarce countries," USAID collaborates with "the public and private sectors to develop and implement new 'water-smart' technologies and seeks opportunities to improve sustainable access to water for 20 million people in the region." Related to this interest in technologies is the privileging of modern communication technologies. A central theme across programs is the projection of technology as central to modernity, using computers to facilitate quality education, business acumen, and even transparent governance. In USAID's description of its work in Egypt, telecommunication networks are included explicitly in its development agenda (2015a).

Advanced technologies foregrounded in development programs also contribute to military action. In addition to addressing the consequences of military intervention in Iraq and Afghanistan, US foreign aid recognizes the regional context in which conflicts and refugees transcend national boundaries. USAID (2015f) attention to the region highlights "crises in Syria, Iraq and Yemen [as] . . . a regional challenge of unparalleled magnitude." The Syrian case illustrates the importance of understanding the millions of refugees, both inside the country and living in Jordan and Lebanon. Documentation of USAID funding for programs in the Arab region demonstrates the recognition of the need for crisis support to Iraq, Syria, West Bank/Gaza, and Yemen, with additional humanitarian support going to Libya and Syria.

Even as US agencies work with individual national governments, an important feature of the geometry (Shah & Wilkins, 2004) visualized in their statements asserts the importance of the region as a whole. Many of the problems described in the overall mission to the MENA region are described as "transnational challenges" in terms of youth unemployment, conflict and extremism, and natural resources such as water (USAID, 2015f). The solution to these challenges is in "increasing private sector investment and enhancing job creation and matching, promoting water security, strengthening local civil society, and advancing gender inclusivity" and promoting "the use of science and technology in regional development" (USAID, 2015f). Asserting the importance of the regional context while privileging free-market economic solutions facilitated through science and technology relies on not only modernization but also neoliberal perspectives.

The foundation of modernization resonates with neoliberal attention to economic growth as the dominant strategic interest guiding development agendas. Moreover, US development visions rely on science and technology as positive forces for social change, particularly when promoting processes to promote economic goals. Economic development focuses on the growth of private business rather than public enterprise connected to the state. USAID projects resonate with this model, describing their work as transformative and beneficial to those individuals who subscribe to their vision of development. The politics of US aid to the region are tied not only to US strategic interests, but also to the perpetuation of global capitalism, as economic frameworks take precedence over more humanitarian concerns. This ideology guiding modernization and neoliberal approaches to development resonates with the broader media landscape in which rescue narratives structure agency and action.

US development discourse concerning its role in the Middle East identifies economic, political, and social problems caused by conflict rooted in traditional culture, potentially solved through more modern technologies afforded through US foreign aid. This foreign aid embodies not just an allocation of financial resources, but also an articulation of social change as instigated through technology toward free-market economic gain and democratic governance promoted largely through modernization strategies. The constructions of development problems, causes, and solutions resonate with the narratives in popular films and games, particularly those devoted to rescue. Connected with the appeal of rescue within the action-adventure genre is a projected delight in acquisition, in the spirit of adventure and on behalf of empire.

Empire Adventure Narrative

Narratives in an action-adventure framework may focus on the adventure, which is justified as central to the project of empire, as well as promote the act of rescue as a significant moment in a sequence of events. These themes allow us to emphasize an analytic distinction between narratives that require a hero to rescue victims from villains in a suspenseful plot, as described above, and narratives that privilege conquest as pleasurable, inevitable, and justifiable, such as *Indiana Jones* (2008). Although less frequently witnessed (12% of the forty-nine films) in this sample, this narrative aligns with action-rescue in terms of its foundation in action-adventure sequences and with magical kingdom in terms of its reliance on myth and mystery.

The object of the conquest may vary, ranging from products and artifacts to whole territories. McAlister (2005) describes the US acquisition of oil and gold as being justified through a narrative that designates these things as universally valued, rather than necessarily owned by individuals and states. The goal of archeology, then, becomes connected with rescuing artifacts from cultures that might not appreciate their value, so that they might be presented to benevolent leaders who would secure them in the interests of humanity. Two relevant films identified in this sample include *Lara Croft: Tomb Raider* (2001) and *National Treasure* (2004). As McAlister (2005) explains, "The great nations are not defined as those that *produce* the greatest art—they are those that *collect* it" (p. 133). And demonstrating the blurred lines between news and fiction, actor Nicolas Cage has recently been interviewed concerning his interest in collecting artifacts, such as a dinosaur skull, in a quest noted as similar to that of his film *National Treasure* (Torres, 2019).

In recent news (Brown, 2019), the British Museum is beginning to return artifacts to Afghanistan and Iraq, recognizing the importance of respecting the cultural heritage of these communities. The performance of museum exhibition thus asserts a legitimacy to maintaining, or returning, these acquisitions. Both *Night at the Museum* films (2006; 2009) incorporate these interests in collecting and exhibiting cultural artifacts.

Another feature identified as integral to those building on empire adventure narratives in these popular films is that the contexts rely on mythical or supernatural creatures, such as mummies and museum dolls. As with the magical kingdom narrative, avoiding realistic characters or plots allows these films to ignore the agency of local communities or history in cultural contexts, thus adding justification for acquisition.

The ubiquitous nature of empire, as an assertion of conventional wisdom through the parameters of our social life, is exemplified by how US communities describe time and space. US standards for measurement still rely on inches, feet, and yards, rooted in British imperialist practice. Greenwich mean time (GMT) is calculated through a Royal Observatory in London, yet it is projected as a "standard" time zone in many areas of the world, particularly in areas connected with the political history of the United Kingdom (such as Australia, India, and South Africa) and by the BBC and various television broadcasting stations in the Arab world, such as the Middle East Broadcasting Center and Al Jazeera. The BBC describes its own history as being initiated with a 1932 "broadcasting to the Empire" (BBC, 2019).

This empire adventure narrative surfaces in popular film. Although the forty-nine films considered relevant from 1996 through 2018 were noted as having some minimal reference to the region, only about one-fifth were designated as including a regional plot or character in some central way. In contrast, two-fifths of these films only referenced the region briefly through landscape. The six films that call adventure and acquisition into play tend to be those related to museums, such as *Night at the Museum* (2006, 2009; see Figure 7), to archeologists, such as *Lara Croft* (2001) as well as *The Mummy* and *The Mummy Returns* (1999, 2001), and to treasure hunters, such as *National Treasure* (2004). The characters that are central to these narratives and positioned as from the Middle East include men such as Imhotep in *Mummy* and Kahmunrah in *Night at the Museum.*

This narrative surfaces in video games as well as films. Games may reference actual events and places, but they lack context with historical depth. Particularly when involving first-person shooters against designated enemies, these game plots consider the Middle East as a background for conflict, such as in *War in the Gulf* and *Delta Force*. A game following a more interactive approach is *Civilization*, though the underlying motives support an imperialist quest. The conflicts tend to be inspired by terrorists taking hostages and threatening the US military (relevant to action rescue), or by supernatural creatures, such as mummies, protecting cultural artifacts (relevant to magical kingdoms). In most of these games, characters identified as from the Middle East were clearly playing the villainous roles; in the few that were not, the characters figured

FIGURE 7. *Night at the Museum: Battle of the Smithsonian* (2009)

more in the background, such as museum guards or groups of bystanders, than as central protagonists. Dawson (2016) likens the "heightened realism" of video games to an emphasis on the "chaotic spaces of global cities in the Middle East" (p. 255), relying on an "imperial gaze" through which an empire engages in visual surveillance of its subjects in order to succeed in colonization.

Not only are regional characters more likely to play negative roles, but also the setting is often passive, thus lacking agency as integral to the plot or central character. For example, Morocco is the setting in which a key agent is killed in *The Bourne Ultimatum* (2007) and serves as a landscape in several other popular films; Dubai sets the stage for a key fighting scene in the earlier *Mission Impossible* (2011); villains are chased through Middle East cities in *Skyfall* (2012), *Iron Man 3* (2013), and *World War Z* (2013); and iconic structures such as the pyramids feature in background shots in *The X-men* (2016). Some of these films only include characters from the Middle East as background figures, such as crowd scenes in both *Transformers* (2009, 2011) films, *GI Joe* (2009), *Taken* (2009, 2012), and *Twilight* (2012). In most of these films, the Middle East serves as background only, a landscape in which people fight or are at least threatening, though they have little voice or consequence to the central plot.

The necessity of conquest emerges through a dichotomized articulation of cultural clash, defining Western nations in terms of idealized enlightenment and democratic civilizations against amorphous terrorists. Dichotomizing tradition from modernity figures in US development discourse as well.

The project of empire is relevant to historical practices that are seen as strengthening Orientalism (Said, 1978). Narratives of development assistance serve to justify foreign aid to other countries through this lens. Other research has demonstrated the importance of neoliberal narratives that legitimate integration into a global capitalist economy and Orientalist narratives that link Northern and Western intervention in Eastern regions (Dutta, 2011; Li, 2007; Willis, Smith, & Stenning, 2008). The particular assertion of Orientalism through a development discourse concerning US aid to the Middle East rests on a framework that juxtaposes "modern" societies against projected "traditional" cultures through access to "modern" media, which at the time of Lerner's (1958) analysis meant radio broadcasts, public screenings of film, and printed news. Lerner's parable of the Turkish village grocer and chief exemplified his privileging of modernity with formal economic assets. While the chief relied on ancestral heritage as his legitimation for authority, the grocer gained value as a broker in trade, privileging cash over a trade economy that offered "modern" items, such as neckties. Clothing tends to be asserted as symbolic of this dichotomized traditional versus modern appearance. The grocer longed to be somewhere else, probably urban, perhaps foreign, while the chief channeled his focus to the local community. The traditional leader relied on obedience to elders, while his more modern counterpart found faith in distant mediated voices calling for national allegiance.

In Lerner's world, modern men (women rarely had a voice or respected visibility in this narrative) rely more on media than on family for information, more on scientific explanations than religious interpretations (Colle, 1989), with more interest in national than local issues. In contrast, the traditional man, most clearly described by Lerner through his presentation of a poor, local peasant with no shoes on his feet, cannot imagine himself anywhere but where he currently stands, resigned to his fate as somehow divinely orchestrated. Glorified mobility through advanced technologies, whether communication or transportation, also feature in popular films, for example, *Men in Black: International* (2019). While the adventure enacted through popular films and games becomes central to guided and witnessed actions, the conception of empire is supported through condescending attributions of cultural traits as traditional and staid in juxtaposition to modern and mobile aspirations.

Magical Kingdom Narrative

The next narrative considered in this analysis projects magical and mythical settings and characters. As with the preceding narratives of action-rescue and empire adventure, this third theme is not mutually exclusive, but integrates elements within the narrative that are not connected with actual contemporary or historical conditions but instead offer a more creative fantasy of supernatural powers and experiences. Examples include *Prince of Egypt* (1998) and *The Mummy* (1999) and *The Mummy Returns* (2001). Even music, exemplified by the Bangles' *Walk Like an Egyptian* (1986), sometimes relies on mythical tropes. Including those films that are also relevant to action rescue, such as *Batman Begins* (2005) and *Wonder Woman* (2017), and empire adventure, about one-third of the forty-nine popular films studied rely on mythical or mystical characterizations. Disentangled from any expectations of realism, current politics are not engaged. This narrative works across films, games, and music in US popular culture.

Relevant to this theme are the many television shows and films devoted to the Aladdin fable (including films in 2009 and 2019). Recent marketing images of the 2019 *Aladdin* contributed to a *Saturday Night Live* "weekend update" skit on May 18, 2019, in which Will Smith's blue-tinted character provoked audience laughter when characterized as a "disturbing image" of evidence for US concern with Iran. Mulder (2019) has critiqued the 2019 version of this film for reducing the "rich complexity" of the Middle East "to a fantasy: simplified place, a backward space . . . that exists only for our visual pleasure." She elaborates that there is a "level of architectural crazy going on in *Aladdin*," akin to having "a film set in medieval Europe that had buildings that were a combination of Greek temples, Viking longhouses, Gothic cathedrals, and Swiss chalets."

Representation of Egypt serves as an illustration of this characterization of the Middle East as mythical in US popular culture. Popular films produced in the United States specifically referencing Egypt include *Gods of Egypt* (2016) and the animated *Prince of Egypt* (1998). The visual references asserted most frequently position Egypt as an ancient culture, heavy with myth and mystery, lacking in currency and complexity. McAlister (2005) differentiates competing perspectives of Egypt within US popular culture, whether positioned as venerable through projected historically based myths, or as vulnerable and thus open to conquest. Some articulations position Egypt as a valuable leader through its position within northern Africa, while others emphasize its proximity to other nations in the Middle East. What both groups share is a mapping of Egypt that preferences constructions that are distant in time and space.

In addition, several depictions of mythologized, ancient Egyptians are released in *The Mummy* (2017; another version in 1999); *The Mummy Returns* (2001); and *The Mummy: Tomb of the Dragon Emperor* (2008). Even in *X Men: Apocalypse* (2016), ancient Egypt surfaces as home to central villain En Sabh Nur, with visual references to veiled women and distant pyramids, as well as audio references to Arabic music. The 2017 production of *The Mummy* with Tom Cruise offers an illustration. The recurring iconic visuals of a pyramid and sphynx were accompanied by familiar images of dark and ancient tombs, beige and dusty deserts, and even the stereotyped evil brunette woman juxtaposed with a wide-eyed, blond heroine. The idea that the central male figures were "insurgents" rather than "looters," who were "liberators of precious antiquities," resonates with the familiar narrative of US agents rescuing valuable artifacts from unappreciative local residents. As the two men ride into a desert scene with their requisite headscarves flying, our central figure derides his sidekick: "Where is your sense of adventure?" (bringing us back to the adventure narrative previously described). Privileging a version of Egypt that relies on the fantastical or the infantile avoids attention to contemporary politics and valuable perspectives. This distancing serves the interests of those who intend to justify acquisition of artifacts, oil, and other resources within the region, relevant to the earlier conquest theme described.

While these cases illustrate the assertion of mythical tropes, other examples foreground conflict. Games based on myths and kingdoms include *Prince of Persia* (2008), fighting against evil; *Tomb Raider: Anniversary* (2007), fighting mummies and acquiring artifacts in Egypt; and *Uncharted 2: Among Thieves* (2009), in which protagonists aim to steal a magical lamp from a museum in Istanbul (these latter two are also relevant to the empire adventure narrative above). Connecting with earlier recognition of conflict in rescue narratives, some of the more violent games are set in historical times, such as *Assassin's Creed* (2007) and *AC: Revelations* (2011), the latter including an American businessman solving mysteries of ancestral plights.

Given that news stories focus on contemporary events, these constructions of the region focus on conflict and are resonant with images of fighting and heroism in popular culture. Development and military intervention run through these themes of conquest and rescue, positioning the superiority of the United States in attempts to justify action and investment. The magical kingdom narrative may not operate explicitly in political and development discourses, but it serves implicitly to support the idea that the communities represented have little connection with contemporary issues. The assertion of the exotic also works to distance the narrative from current concerns or connections.

Historical Drama and Other Narrative Approaches

Historical dramas are just barely visible in this set of films, but they are worth considering given their resonance across popular culture. Three popular films rely on historical settings and stories to situate characters in dramas: *Gladiator* (2000), *The Passion of the Christ* (2004), and *300* (2007). Even with Mel Gibson's controversial pronouncements, *The Passion of the Christ* (2004) was widely viewed, matching trends documented with earlier biblical dramas, such as *Exodus* (1960). Images marketing the other films are strikingly like those of historically situated video games. In *300* (2007), for example, Greek Spartans fight against Persian villains, with positioning, costuming, and shading similar to the marketing copy for games.

Although the connection between Freddie Mercury and the Middle East seems tangential, hired research assistants deemed the film *Bohemian Rhapsody* (2018) relevant in a minor way, given the central figure's Persian roots and his family's Zoroastrian religion, and having been born in Zanzibar at a time (1946) when part of the British Empire contributed to these connections. Although the connection to the Middle East is barely visible within this narrative, a projection of Persian heritage contributes to family tension as Mercury navigates his identity in this biographically based drama. While this film engages historically recognized stories of this musical celebrity, Michael Moore's documentary *Fahrenheit 9/11* (2004) explicates historical events such as the US intervention in Iraq and political analyses of powerful networks linking the Bush family with the Saud regime. This documentary highlights the Middle East in problematic ways, simultaneously positing the region as a place of deceit and manipulation in the case of Saudi Arabia and ripe for military engagement in the case of Iraq.

Enduring Narratives

Given an array of potential genres and a possibility of varied sequences, narratives building from action-adventure and concentrating on rescue missions and adventurously driven conquests endure. The idea that violence is inevitable, proliferated in news stories, development polices, films, games, and more, helps to build a justification for these interventions. Yet, even with the dominance and endurance of these key themes, there appear to be small but significant shifts over time in US media.

In news coverage, topics covering violence eclipsed attention to politics in 2001, 2006, and again 2014–2015. The year 2001 was a significant juncture in US history and in regional violence, with much of the national press concentrating on coverage of 9/11 and the subsequent "war on terrorism" (Fleck & Kilby, 2010). Also relevant this year was increased conflict between Israelis and Palestinians. Accentuated coverage in 2006 built on the capture and execution of Saddam Hussein, illustrating the victorious acts of the United States as heroic in the face of projected villainy. A later rise in coverage in 2014–15 addressed violence in Israel and Gaza, along with the rise of Daesh.

In the years around 9/11, US news concerning the Middle East was much more likely than in other years to originate in the United States. Considering subjects over time, dominance of attention to Israeli and Palestinian issues prior to 9/11 has subsided since. Attention to Israel in the news fell from 37 percent in 1996–2001 to 28 percent in subsequent years, with a similar though less dramatic trend in decreasing attention to Palestinian issues (19%–15%). Attention to Egypt was also less prominent over time, with more attention to Iraq, due to intensified US military intervention there.

As direct military engagement intensified in the post-9/11 era, there was a proportional reliance on action and adventure in popular film. Overall, the percentage of films referencing the Middle East and featuring rescue themes rose from under half (43%) to two-thirds (64%) in the post-9/11 era. Before 9/11, two of the films referencing the region, though through very minor plots and settings, were comedies, while no comedies in these top-twenty popularity lists have done so since. What has endured is the prevalence of empire adventure (including films from 1999 through 2009).

Themes relevant to both rescue missions and mystical settings in the Middle East appear to become more often positioned within popular films over time. Only three films in the earliest six years do so, but in the post-9/11 era, particularly since 2012, this tendency increases. Moreover, films with historical settings in the region, including historical dramas, were more likely to appear pre-9/11; the historical dramas themselves feature on these lists between 2000 and 2007.

Attention to plots and settings, as well as inclusion of major characters (about one-quarter) from the region, do not demonstrably change over the time period considered. Neither does the propensity to exclude characters from the region as heroes. What has changed is a growing inclusion of characters from the region serving as victims and as villains in the post-9/11 era. Overall, characters identified with the region were much more likely to be villains and victims than heroes, and when positively portrayed protagonists, these characters were more likely to be included in magical kingdom narratives than plots rooted in expectations of realistic adventures. Overall, then, those with agency were less likely to be included than those with vulnerability, thereby justifying the inevitable rescue and adventurous conquest.

Considering trends over time, the year 2001 marks a significant juncture in US history, with subsequent years accentuating explicit intervention in Iraq and actions against Daesh. Development investments followed military interventions with increased funding. These events and decisions moved what had been a high concentration of news concerning Israeli and Palestinian concerns to other areas within the region. And the rise of Daesh corresponded with more attention to victims and fewer heroes in popular culture narratives.

Narrating the Middle East

Building on the foundation of a focus on violence and conflict, particularly through US television news, popular culture and official development policies rely on narratives that justify US heroic intervention to save despairing victims from desperate villains. Related to the rescue of people, narratives of conquest justify acquisition, assuming passivity among local communities and universality of value, whether art, artifact, or oil. When people identified with the region are portrayed in a more positive light, they tend to be featured in narratives of myths and magic, distancing agency from contemporary contexts. While these narratives endure over time, it is worth noting that since 9/11 we see an accentuated presence of action-adventure themes in popular culture, with attendant privileging of youth and their expertise with advanced technologies in discourses of development agencies and news media.

A narrative of an American masculine hero justifies intervention on behalf of victims, typically women and children who are in despair due to constructed cultural values, whether in fiction, news stories, or development activities; the hero resolves the strife caused by outmoded traditions by bringing new technologies to suffering people (Wilkins, 2004). Recognizing the gendered portrayal of rescue, technologies play a central role in heroic practice. When people from the Middle East are featured as heroic, narratives rely on characteristics that are considered as aligning with the projected values and appearances dominant in the United States. The framing of prominent Palestinian politician and political leader Hanan Ashrawi illustrates this key point (Wilkins, 1995). The heroes of the tale in US news coverage of Egyptian protests (Ghobrial & Wilkins, 2015) are the attractive and technologically savvy youth, resonant with a Western audience in terms of their appearance and projected exuberance, working to thwart the villainous older men who victimize women and children. Following the trajectory of this narrative, authors of this mediated discourse conclude their tales with visions of crowds cheering as the nominal leader steps away from office. Emphasis on the contrived event of Saddam Hussein's statue being toppled in Iraq illustrates the symbolic import of this as media event, meant to complete the tale rather than recognize that political transition requires much more than a change in leadership.

Women tend to be presented in passive more than active roles, strengthening the idea that they need to be rescued, whether in news, film, or development narratives (Wilkins, 2015). Wilson's (2011) analysis of the images of women used in publicity campaigns to raise funding for Oxfam, Nike, and other organizations confirms considerable scholarship demonstrating this passivity. Moreover, when women are active, they are coded as such through their entrepreneurship and their connection to technologies, further reinforcing neoliberal globalization (Wilkins, 1997).

It is this gendered rescue fantasy that grounds justification for the asserted role of the United States as a benevolent and necessary masculine hero in the context of Middle East crises and concerns. And what enables these heroic feats is faith in the power of communications and technologies to command modernization in the form of free-market economies and democratic elections.

It is striking that across these narratives the Middle East comes to signify more landscape than human agency, particularly in empire adventure narratives. In many action-adventure films and games, cities identified within the Middle East serve as visual context for scenes that involve serious direct combat or other threatening situations. When agency is granted in the form of a major character, these figures are decidedly more often evil than virtuous or heroic. In the context of the action-adventure narrative permeating games and films, the victims in Middle East settings cannot save themselves, but require rescue from US military forces or corporate men with combat or technological expertise (such as *Iron Man 3* (2013).

Development and news attention are drawn not only by the social problems considered worthy of recognition, but also by celebrities engaged in public relations and strategic communication, such as Matt Damon advocating for clean water, Peter Gabriel for human rights, and Angelina Jolie for children. Celebrities leverage their status to raise awareness of particular issues to support fundraising for causes and foundations and to access leading politicians and powerful people. Their connections to global economic elite are well documented, as are their activities in global development projects (Cooper, 2008; Kapoor, 2013; Tsaliki et al., 2001; Wilkins, 1995). In the case of media attention to the Middle East, one actor, Tom Cruise, contributes to these portrayals through multiple fronts.

American Made (2017), based on a true story, and the mythical *Mummy* (2016), both utilized the star power of celebrity Tom Cruise, but neither made it to the top twenty in the year of their releases. But given the direct connection each of these films has with this discussion of mediated representation, it is worth considering Cruise's role as a US operative. Bored with conventional work as a pilot, he agrees to work with the CIA to avoid drug smuggling charges. His CIA counterpart explains that the work is "America at its finest! We're building nations!" in that they are engaging in surveillance over the "enemies of democracy." Music and landscape position this sequence in the 1970s and 1980s. Most of the plot is based in the Americas, but references are made to the Middle East when Israel confiscates Russian AK-47s from the PLO and when someone suggests that they turn to Iran for assistance with arms transfers. Here, just as in the more popular film series *Mission Impossible: Ghost Protocol* (2011), *Mission Impossible: Rogue Nation* (2015), and *Mission Impossible: Fallout* (2018; see Figure 8), with Tom Cruise again as white American hero battling for launch codes with Dubai as scenery, the Middle East serves as passive landscape for action and adventure.

Celebrity status may offer a vehicle for shifting the norms that limit media representation, though individual agency may be confronted with the weight of institutional systems and policies. Rami

FIGURE 8. *Mission Impossible: Fallout* (2018)

Malek, award-winning actor recently known for his starring role in *Bohemian Rhapsody* (2018), gave public interviews establishing his decision to play a villain in an upcoming *Bond* film, provided that the character would not be identified as Arab or as Muslim (Feuerherd, 2019; MSN Entertainment, 2019). Asserting pride as a first-generation Egyptian American, Malek is able to voice his critique of Hollywood conventions that equate terrorism with the Middle East.

While Malek has been able to leverage his status to have a public voice, *Star Wars: Rogue One* (2018) and *Sound of Metal* (2020) star Riz Ahmed's stop at the US border on his way to a film event in Chicago is a reminder that systems of control still structure individual mobility (Gelt, 2019). Coverage of this Homeland Security stop did give Ahmed voice in that he was able to say that being identified as "Muslim" was quite "scary." But like Malek, recently Oscar-nominated Ahmed also refers to his familiarity with prejudice and discrimination.

These cases draw attention to the ways in which individuals may attempt to advocate to change dominant narratives in US media, as well as the challenges engaged. How we might envision and enact advocacy is discussed in the final chapter. Next, I explore consequences of dominant narratives rooted in action adventure.

4 *Mediating the Middle East*

Given the prevalence and endurance of dominant narratives and constructed maps of the "Middle East," next I explore their consequences in US society. The overarching question concerns how media shape political attitudes by accentuating prejudice and fear of violence in certain dominant and enduring narratives. Following a summary of how US media project constructions of Arab, Muslim, and Middle Eastern communities, I articulate a mediation process as a way of understanding how these narratives become understood and interpreted in political sensibilities.

As established in earlier chapters, this project confirms previous scholarship documenting anti-Arab and anti-Muslim sentiment in US media. Dominant narratives portray the United States as heroically rescuing women and children in the face of projected violence from Arab and Muslim men. Given the extensive documentation of problematic stereotypes and narratives, it is important that we explore their consequences with regard to attitudes and experiences in US communities.

Mediating Prejudice

The process of mediating suggests that the intentions embedded in the production of media content may be reshaped through a collective production and distribution of texts, negotiated and understood within social, cultural, and political contexts. Considering this process of interpretation as a "prism" engages a metaphor that considers refraction and dispersion as consequences of the emanation of light, given particular angles and surfaces. We move beyond a simplistic understanding of media effects as clear reflection by foregrounding the complex ways that preexisting identities and ideas, filtering norms and opportunities, condition responses to mediated narratives. That the angles and surfaces of a prism determine the potential dispersal of wavelengths projected through it, a constructed shape, allows us to construe the optical nature of communication as a structural and contextual process that is adaptable through human action, but also subject to resistance given the capacity to reshape these prisms. Political prisms become more challenging to reshape in public discourse when mediated stereotypes limit the potential for compassion and connection, particularly when people lack direct familiarity or experience with other communities.

Cultural studies scholarship has referenced these frameworks of integrated hostilities as a "prism" in a variety of contexts. Rada and Wulfemeyer (2005), in one illustration, consider how bias in sportscasting is revealed through a "prism of race" (p. 68). As a way of conceptualizing an intersection between race and gender, scholars have asserted these prejudices as a prism (Johnson & Loscocco, 2015) of "racialized gender knowledge" that structures media presentations (Kaler, 2010). Others highlight Islamophobia as a particular "prism" that frames news stories (Marzano, 2011) or popular culture, as a way to project collective anxiety and paranoia (Werbner, 2013). In Gilroy's (2012) work, the concept of a prism brings together fear of Islamic extremism with anxiety over immigration and racism. Building from these frameworks, I articulate an integrated set of prejudices as a prism that contributes to and draws from dominant media stereotypes.

Recognizing the distinct nature of categorizations that reference religious affiliation, ancestral background, and territorial residence, this research explores attitudes and experiences within the United States as well as perceptions of the Middle East and global threats. This approach extends from Said's (1978) articulation of Orientalism, adding complexity in asserting that cultural dominance not only shapes American perceptions of communities outside of the West, but also filters through tensions within the United States. Key here is understanding Orientalism as a hegemonic process that reinforces power structures through the subjugation of communities coded as "Middle Eastern" (Park & Wilkins, 2005). Building on these studies, I question whether engagement with media, particularly action-adventure tropes, contributes to the fear of violence from the Middle East. Moreover, I question whether attraction to this genre also contributes to the fear of terrorism more broadly.

Mediating Attitudes

Concerns with problematic content rely on assumptions that media have some effect on public attitudes and practices. There is a wealth of research considering the relationship between content and consequence that confirms these concerns.

First, negative portrayals limit the potential for sympathetic attitudes among those who do not identify with the projected communities (Tukachinsky et al., 2015). Action-adventure films become particularly affecting for those with little experience or knowledge of Arab culture, thus limiting knowledge of the region, contributing to prejudice, and implanting the belief that these films portray a "realistic" vision of Arab communities (Wilkins, 2008). This sense of perceived realism may condition audience engagement with fictional narratives, whether considering internal coherence within a narrative or a projected consistency between fictional and actual realities (Busselle & Bilandzic, 2008). In surveys of non-Muslim US college students, Saleem et al. (2015) conclude that those with no direct experience rely on media, and they are more likely to perceive Muslims as aggressive and to support military action in Muslim countries. White non-Muslim Americans hold more negative views of Muslim Americans than do other groups, including African Americans and Hispanics; moreover, those who carry these discriminatory views are more likely to support public spending on defense, border security, and the "war on terror" (Sides and Gross, 2013). Other research confirms correlations between negative media content and attitudes connecting Islam with terrorism (Park et al., 2007).

Second, negative portrayals may also influence those who are being stereotyped. Arab American viewers find media stereotypes immensely offensive and difficult to negotiate, notably when traveling through airports (Wilkins, 2008). Tukachinsky et al. (2017) exhibit correlations between type of portrayal (positive or negative) and sense of identity among African American and Latinx communities. More work needs to be done to link documented discrimination and harassment with problematic media narratives, particularly in Arab American and Muslim American communities.

In light of these studies, I examine the question of whether engagement with media promotes prejudice against Arab or Muslim communities. Moreover, I explore the extent to which this connection may be mediated through personal identity and experience, thus accentuating the impact of media on audiences that do not connect with characterizations or narratives. In this specific project, identity with Arab or Muslim heritage and experience with these communities serve as the focus.

Identities and Experience

Resonant identities, such as self-identification as Arab or as Muslim, are expected to serve as antecedent conditions that guide media reception. Studies of Arab American youth have documented serious bullying and discrimination, leading to concerns about stress and self-esteem (Albdour et al., 2017; Tabbah et al., 2016). Some actively hide their Arab identities in the face of hostility within the United States by changing names, accents, and clothing (Naber, 2014). Muslim and Arab Americans have had their citizenship publicly and routinely questioned (Akram, 2002; Alsultany, 2012; Selod, 2015), as the rate of violent crimes against these groups increased dramatically following 9/11 (ADC, 2008). These experiences of discrimination are exacerbated through media representations that limit social dynamics as well as public perceptions (Tukachinsky, 2015).

The role of media in the formation of political attitudes is expected to be conditioned by direct experience. In this study, direct experience in the Middle East is shown to be able to intervene between media engagement and fear of the region, while experience with hate crimes may also mitigate the effects of media on prejudicial attitudes.

Research Approach

This study explores the connection between popular culture engagement and attitudes toward Arab and Muslim communities and the Middle East. These perspectives are differentiated in terms of sentiments and experiences within the United States and fear of the Middle East and of terrorism. The analyses build on cross-sectional comparisons, contrasting Arab and Muslim Americans with other US citizens.

This research relies on national survey data of US adults, based on an instrument designed by the author and approved through University Institutional Review Board procedures, given informed consent and other ethical practices. Zogby Analytics was commissioned to implement this online survey June 7–9, 2017. A sample of US adults, with an additional quota sample of Arab Americans, was selected based on Zogby Analytics' networks of research participants to build a broad and diverse participant list. Respondents were randomly selected from these lists and invited to participate in the survey. Standard practices to ensure anonymity and integrity were followed. Using a variety of other data sources, including census, voter registration, and other demographics, results were weighted to improve proportional representation to approximate US citizens broadly and Arab American citizens specifically. Strategic over-sampling of Arab Americans allowed the intended comparisons for questions raised in this cross-sectional research approach. However, given reliance on non-probability selection processes, it would not be appropriate to generalize the results based on these findings. Instead, the value of the work lies in the contrasts enabled within a cross-sectional research design.

The survey included 1,416 respondents. Given intentional sampling procedures designed to reach a higher proportion of this community, almost one-third of this sample (29%; $n = 410$) identified as Arab American. This group was asked to indicate their heritage, listing sixteen Arab countries, the most prevalent being Egypt (24%), Morocco (11%), Lebanon (10%), Saudi Arabia (9%), and the United Arab Emirates (9%), with smaller proportional representation from other territories. These Arab American respondents represented diverse religious affiliations, identifying mostly with Christian (26%) and Muslim (30%) faiths. Although there is a correlation between Arab and Muslim identities ($r = .34, p < .01$), it is important to recognize diversities within these communities: within the broader sample, only 8 percent were both Muslim and Arab, while another 21 percent were Arab but not Muslim and 3 percent Muslim but not Arab.

These respondents included a diverse range of ethnic, religious, and political identities. When asked their ethnicity, most identified as Caucasian (59%), Arab (10%), Hispanic (9%), or African American (8%), as well as other identities, such as Asian, Native American, and multiracial.[1] Documented religious affiliations included Catholic (24%), Protestant (15%), Evangelical (10%), Muslim (9%), Jewish (4%), Mormon (2%), Hindu (2%), and Buddhist (1%), with others declaring atheism (7%) or no affiliation.

Respondents ranged in age from eighteen to ninety-one (median age was forty-six), with 52 percent identifying as female and 47 percent as male. Few of these respondents had not completed high school (3%), with 21 percent acquiring this certification as their highest degree, another 26 percent had some college experience, and most had graduated from college (38%) or received postgraduate degrees (14%). Annual family incomes were split roughly into thirds, delineating those with annual family incomes less than $35,000 (29%); $35,000–$74,999 (38%); and at least $75,000 (33%). Education and income were combined ($r = .34$, $p < .01$) into an approximation of socioeconomic status (SES), resulting in one-third designated in relatively lower (29%), more than half in middle (57%), and fewer in higher (14%) rankings.

Direct experiences in the Middle East and experiences with discrimination in the United States were expected to mitigate media effects, such that those without these experiences might be more likely to be influenced by mediated narratives. These scales were created by the author with specific interests relevant to this study. Responses ranged from strongly agree to strongly disagree on a five-point scale of categorizations.

Experience in the Middle East

About one-fifth (21%) of the respondents had traveled to the Middle East or had family currently living in the Middle East (20%). To approximate this connection, these two variables are included with a third factor indicating interest in traveling to the Middle East (alpha = .69; Eigenvalue = 2.0 with the first variable predicting 49% of variance in factor analysis). About one-third of the sample (32%) expressed this affinity for the region. It is worth including this as a distinct variable separate from identity as Arab or Muslim, given the diversity within the region and connections with Iran, Israel, and Turkey. Direct experience in the region was more likely among those who are Arab ($r = .49, p < .01$), Muslim ($r = .31, p < .01$), and wealthier ($r = .13, p < .01$). It was expected that those with direct experience and interest in the region would be less likely to fear the Middle East.

Hate Crime Experience in the United States

The study shows that experience with hate crimes may result in more sympathetic attitudes toward others facing discrimination. A scale of experience with hate crimes and prejudice in the United States included level of agreement to these statements: I have experienced discrimination in the US because of my ethnicity or race; I have experienced harassment in the US; I know someone who has been racially profiled in the US. This scale produced an alpha of .82 with an Eigenvalue of 2.2 with the first of three variables predicting 74 percent of the variance. The distribution resulted in a mean of 9.4, close to the median of 9, showing a differentiation of categories of agreement, meaning more likely to have experienced hate crimes and discrimination (33%) from those who were less committal (26%) and those who disagreed, or did not have these experiences themselves or among people they knew (41%). It is expected that this experience with hate crimes would foster empathic concern with others facing prejudice within the United States.

Focusing on those who documented their experience with hate crimes in the United States (those who agreed to these statements), Arab Americans were much more likely to experience or know someone who has been a victim of a hate crime (61%, compared with 21%; $r = .38$, $p < .01$), as were Muslim Americans (59% compared with 29%; $r = .20$, $p < .01$). It is important also to note the stark differences in other ethnic identities as well: although only 15 percent of European American respondents reported having this experience or knowing someone who has, this proportion was much higher among African American (60%), Asian American (55%), Hispanic (44%), multiracial (60%), and Native American respondents (42%). Across cultural identifications within the United States, there was a marked difference in hate crime experience among those not of European descent.

Media Engagement

Most respondents said they spend time engaging with popular culture, particularly television (83% watching at least one program on the day prior to the survey); film (46% watching at least one film on the day prior to the survey); and videogames (41% playing a game on the day prior to the survey). Most also enjoy action-adventure films (76%). Given the centrality of action-adventure to this research project, other questions on this subject were included. These respondents tended to agree that action-adventure is an enjoyable genre, though they were more evenly split as to whether these films "portray realistic events" or whether they identify with heroes. Five variables contributed to a scale of action-adventure engagement, including experience watching films and playing videogames, liking action adventure, identifying with heroes, and believing in the genre's realism (alpha = .73; Eigenvalue = 2.5 with first component predicting 50% of the variance). This scale was coded to differentiate those with more engagement (33%) from those with less.

Those identifying as Arab were less likely to be fans of action adventure (11%) than others (42%, $r = -.30$, $p < .01$), with similar trends among those identifying as Muslim (21% fans compared with 34%, $r = -.09$, $p < .01$). Men were more likely to engage with action adventure than women ($r = .07$, $p < .01$), though there was no difference across socioeconomic status. It was expected that this media engagement would matter most in predicting attitudes among those who did not have direct experience or identification with problematized communities or territories.

Attitudes

The following attitudinal scales represent opinions about US citizens distinct from those concerning the Middle East and terrorism. These scales were created by the author in order to approximate specific interests in assessing attitudes toward Arab and Muslim communities within and outside the United States. Responses ranged from strongly agree to strongly disagree on five-point categorizations.

ANTI-ARAB AND ANTI-MUSLIM PREJUDICE IN THE UNITED STATES

The scale addressing specific discrimination in the United States included level of agreement to these statements: Prejudice against Arab Americans is a serious concern in the US; I know someone of Arab ethnicity or with an Arabic-speaking background who has experienced discrimination in the US; I know someone who is Muslim and has experienced discrimination in the US; Islam is a peaceful religion. These four variables contribute to an alpha of .83 and an Eigenvalue of 2.7 with the first of four variables predicting 66 percent of the variance. A normal distribution of this scale matches the mean and median at 12, distinguishing a categorization of agreement (37%) from more neutral (25%) and disagreement, meaning more prejudice against Arab and Muslim Americans (38%).

Not surprisingly, the study found that those with no hate crime experience are more likely to host these discriminatory attitudes (66%, compared with 25%; $r = -.38$, $p < .01$) than those with no direct experience in the Middle East region ($r = -.38$, $p < .01$). Although there was no documented difference across socioeconomic status, men were more likely to exhibit this prejudice than women ($r = .07$, $p < .05$), as were non-Muslim respondents (67%, compared to 33% of others; $r = -.17$, $p < .01$) and non-Arab Americans (72%, compared to 23% of others; $r = -.38$, $p < .01$).

FEAR OF THE MIDDLE EAST

The next attitudinal variable assesses fear of the Middle East region, considering an expected threat of violence. This scale includes levels of agreement to the following statements: the main enemies of the US are based in the Middle East; most of the terrorist acts in the US are committed by Arabs; the Middle East is a dangerous region; and the US should expand military involvement in the Middle East. These four variables create a reliable (alpha = .67) and valid (Eigenvalue of 2.0 with first factor predicting 51% of variance) scale. Given a normal distribution (both mean and median at 11 points in a 20-point scale), this variable was recoded for agreement on these factors (53%), contrasted with others disagreeing or not registering an opinion. This attitude is not correlated with Arab or Muslim identity, with direct experience in the region, or with socioeconomic status. However, gender (with men feeling more threatened; $r = .12, p < .01$) does play a role.

FEAR OF TERRORISM

A general fear of danger in the world making the United States less safe was assessed through a scale of levels of agreement to these statements: the world is a dangerous place; terrorism is a major threat in the US; I am anxious about potential terrorist threats; people in the US face serious terrorism threats. Answers to these questions produce a scale with an alpha of .78 and an Eigenvalue of 2.4 with the first of four variables predicting 61 percent of the variance. A normal distribution curve with matching mean and median at 9 helped differentiate those with higher levels of fear (34%) from those more neutral (33%) and those with less concern (33%). This attitude did not appear to be related to direct experience or Arab or Muslim identity. Fear of terrorism in general did correlate with fear of the Middle East ($r = .29, p < .01$).

Consequences of Action-Adventure Engagement

This section focuses on the degree to which action-adventure engagement may be associated with prejudicial attitudes. Following consideration of bivariate relationships between media engagement and attitudes, analyses explore the degree to which these patterns might be accentuated across those given resonant identities and experiences. These analyses use three-way cross-tabulations to consider patterns, as well as regression analyses to consider the relative contributions of these individual factors with standardized beta coefficients, documenting significance at the level of $p < .01$.

Anti-Arab and Anti-Muslim Prejudice in the United States

Action-adventure fans are more likely to exhibit prejudice, contrasting over half (53%) compared with 30 percent of those who are not fans (gamma = .43; $p<.01$). This distinction becomes more pronounced when differentiating those who identify as Muslim or as Arab. The groups most likely to hold these discriminatory attitudes are non-Muslim (81%), and non-Arab fans (84%). In sharp contrast, only 26 percent of Muslim and 28 percent of Arab respondents engaging with these media hold this prejudice.

Recognizing a correlation between identity and hate crime experience, those who do not experience discrimination but do actively engage with action-adventure genres are much more likely to exhibit prejudice (50%) than those who avoid the genre but are familiar with hate crimes (8%). However, the difference is less prominent among those who do not relate to hate crimes whether a fan of action adventure (50%) or not (46%; gamma = .23, $p < .01$), whereas this media engagement does differentiate among those with hate crime experience between fans (25%) and those who are not fans (8%; gamma = .57, $p < .01$).

The study found that this prejudice is not related to socioeconomic status but is more likely among male (41%) than female (35%) respondents. Being an action-adventure fan almost doubles the likelihood of prejudice among men (64% of male fans, compared to 32% of their male counterparts; gamma = -.57, $p < .01$), with a more moderate but present effect on women (45% of female fans, compared to 29% of their female counterparts; gamma = .33,

TABLE 4. Impact of Action-Adventure Engagement

	Prejudice in the US	Fear of the Middle East	Fear of Terrorism
Media Engagement	.08*	.09*	.11*
Arab Identity	-.26*	-.04	.01
Muslim Identity	.01	-.03	-.02
Hate crime experience	-.27*		
Direct experience		.03	
Gender		-.11*	
Adjusted R Squared	.22	.02	.01
SE	.43	.50	.81

Note: B* weights from topic-specific regression analyses.
* $p < .001$

p < .01). Action-adventure then has a more pronounced effect on prejudice among men, though still contributing to women's prejudice who actively are consuming this genre.

Relying on regression analyses, the strongest predictors of this prejudice are those who do not identify as Arab and do not have hate crime experience, with a significant contribution from those who do engage with action adventure (see Table 4). Given that SES and gender do not have independent effects on this attitude, the multivariate analyses focus on assessing the relative contribution of media engagement in light of identity and experience. In this study, identity as Muslim does not predict lack of prejudice, but experience with discrimination, itself correlated with Arab identity, does matter; without this experience and identity, media consumption contributes to the likelihood of this prejudice.

Fear of the Middle East

Next, analyses consider the relative contribution of direct experience in the region, along with identities and media engagement, in predicting fear of the Middle East. Given that gender and SES appear to be connected with this fear, these variables are included in this regression.

Those who engage with action-adventure are more likely to fear the Middle East (61%) than those do not (47%; gamma = .28, $p < .01$). This perspective appears more likely among fans, whether Muslim (58%) or not (62%), and whether Arab (61%) or not (62%). Those without direct experience are more similar in their perceptions (51% of non-fans compared with 56% of fans), whereas only 35 percent of those who are not fans and have experience find the region threatening, but action-adventure engagement increases this concern to 67 percent.

Gender matters in this equation as well, with more male (60%) compared with female (48%) respondents registering fear of the Middle East (gamma = -.23, $p < .01$). Given that gender is correlated with action-adventure experience (gamma = .15, $p < .01$), it is useful to consider the relative contribution of these factors through multivariate analyses. Socioeconomic status bears a moderate relationship with this attitude (gamma = .13, $p < .01$).

Including these factors into a regression equation, the strongest significant predictor of this fear is action-adventure media engagement (see Table 4). This is a striking result, in that direct experience and identity become obscure, with media dominating as a predicting factor, along with gender, noting that men are both more likely to be action-adventure fans and to be concerned with potential terrorist threats from the Middle East.

Fear of Terrorism

Next, I consider fear of terrorism in general, which correlates with fear of the Middle East ($r = .29, p < .01$; see Table 4). Action-adventure fans are more likely to be concerned with terrorism in the United States in general (46%, compared with 25% of those who are not fans; $r = -.59, p < .01$). This relationship does not appear to be mediated by identity as Muslim (46% non-Muslim fans and 47% of Muslim fans share this fear), although those who identify as Arab and do not consume this genre are much less likely to worry about terrorism (16%, compared with 27% of those who are not Arab and not fans, whereas this sentiment is shared by 45% of non-Arabs and 46% Arab fans). As with fear of the Middle East, when considering these factors together the sole predictor of concern with terrorism is that of media engagement.

Mediating the Middle East

Action-adventure engagement becomes a more salient predictor of political attitudes that concern global threats, though they are predicated on experience and Arab identity in considering prejudice within the United States. Particularly with the more distanced threat of violence, consumers of this genre are more likely to confirm the dominant narratives that assert violence and villains as emanating from the Middle East.

When considering discriminatory attitudes within the United States, we see dramatic differences across identification with Arab communities, as well as those with direct experience with hate crimes, though these attributes themselves are connected. Significantly, we find competing worlds, with few European Americans

(15%) registering hate crime experience compared with more than half of those identifying with other ethnic affiliations. Identification as Arab within the US community appears to be a stronger factor in predicting lack of prejudice than an affiliation with Islam.

Overall, action-adventure fans appear more threatened by their conception of the Middle East, regardless of their heritage or affiliation, though this fear is dramatically reduced among those with direct experience in the region. Before concluding that this form of media engagement contributes to prejudice against the Middle East specifically, however, it is worth situating this threat as related to a broader fear of terrorism. Action-adventure fans are much more concerned than others over the risk of terrorism within the United States, regardless of identity or experience. The consequence of increased exposure and interest in these identified narratives, then, may be more relevant to a general sense of fear.

As expected, direct experiences and relevant identities influence perspectives related to prejudice, but these characteristics have little to do with perception of terrorist threat. In the absence of experience or proximity, media play a critical role in contributing to fear, particularly when dominant narratives accentuate perceptions of threat and need for security.

Action-adventure media reinforce problematic stereotypes, perpetuating prejudice and fear. These enduring representations remain problematic. Given the correlations across these discriminatory attitudes, it is worth noting the different ways media engagement influences this reception. Internal prejudice is related to fear of the Middle East ($r = .20, p < .01$), though not to fear of terrorism more broadly, though fear of the Middle East and of terrorism bear a strong correlation ($r = .29, p < .01$). These attitudes may be seen as constituting a spectrum from a more localized prejudice (within the United States) to a regional prejudice (view of the Middle East), then to a more abstract fear of global terrorism; the first and third attitudes are not connected, but there are significant links between internal and external prejudice, and fear of the Middle East and of the world.

The central contribution of this analysis is to demonstrate clear links between engagement with action-adventure and these discriminatory attitudes and fears. Previous chapters chronicling problematic stereotypes in US media raise critical questions concerning the potential consequences of these characterizations. Rising public hate within the United States demands attention to the conditions that provoke and perpetuate this discrimination.

Understanding the way mediated narratives contribute to political attitudes may allow us to consider next options for improving our media and our communities. It is worth considering the extent to which more sympathetic characters and narratives might support more compassionate perspectives. Strategies for addressing these concerns are explored in the next chapter.

5 *Visioning from the US Prism*

In this concluding chapter I integrate the results of the mapping, narrating, and mediating analyses to offer a comprehensive critique of US media constructions of the region known in this context as the Middle East. Following this review of the study's findings, I propose communication literacy as an approach to intervention that may enable empathy and build critique.

Media matter: it is not just one film, or a single news story, but an avalanche of media reproducing dominant themes that contribute to our internal socialization, our daily experiences, and our global politics. Relying on mediation as a theoretical foundation in communication scholarship, I position this work not as a critique of just the texts themselves, but of their centrality within social norms, political decisions, and cultural interpretations. These media impose a particularly masculine and nationalist version of US citizenship upon popular culture, news, and foreign policies, despite the diverse ancestries and religious alliances that compose the US populace.

The argument of this project is that US-based communications, including a variety of discourses and platforms, mediate the Middle East in ways that implicate an underlying prejudice and inspire fear. US prisms of mediated narratives build on positioned perspectives, situating communities as "Middle" and "East" through constructed mapping as territories are articulated and engaged. The analyses have described how US discourse articulates mapping and positions narratives, with consequences for prevailing perceptions.

The United States Mapping the Middle East

In chapter 2, I explore articulations of the Middle East present in public discourse through US agencies, news, and popular culture. Positioning these constructions within the perspective of the United States, we understand the privileging of observations that explicitly characterize this region as "East." This politically grounded assertion manifests in projected and simplistic constructions that permeate public and popular discourse, erasing the diversity within Middle Easter communities. The power to name a territory clearly rests with the elite controlling the production of knowledge, contributing to moral geographies that appear as more factual than merely institutionally constructed and perpetuated.

The specific definition of which countries constitute the Middle East varies by agency and author, and other terms, such as *Western Asia*, demonstrate how alternatives are presented through other institutional projects. More recent articulations of a "New Middle East" bring attention to territories of value and interest to the United States, including Iran, Turkey, and Afghanistan.

Official US agencies engage in development work in much of this region, with trade being more extensive with the wealthier states, particularly those connected with global capital, and military intervention driving the definition of the region in an eastern direction. Official funding tends to follow military intervention, and additional countries are identified for exceptional financial assistance based on their political alliances with the US government. Iraq and Afghanistan are framed as requiring rescue, while parts of the Levant are celebrated as entrepreneurial for their technological skill and success in capitalist enterprise.

Most of the television news reviewed in the study focused on Israeli and Palestinian sites and concerns, particularly pre-9/11, bringing more visibility to the Levant than other areas in the region. News coverage also features Iraq and Afghanistan quite frequently, particularly in terms of violence and US military intervention, given the focus for this research project on the stories that explicitly refer to the "Middle East" in their texts. This sample of mainstream news emphasizes violence and threat over economic progress or social achievements. American perspectives are accentuated, as the majority of sites and (dominantly male) journalists are based in the United States.

Violence is featured in much of the news discourse about the Middle East, similar to its appearance in popular culture. US popular films mostly reference the cultural geography of the region through visual landscape, which is a relatively minor aspect of the plot, often in scenes of confrontation.

In the photographs presented on public digital sites produced by USAID, similar to other discourses, attention to women and girls prevails, describing them conventionally as students, youth, and refugees grateful for US development assistance. When men are pictured, they tend to be described through their political and professional positions.

Visual images used to market popular games and films also contribute to a construction of characters and themes articulating the positioning of the Middle East. The games referencing this region tend to rely on conflict as the motivating interaction or on mythical settings. As with films, signs in Arabic in scenery are used to indicate location. Pharaohs and pyramids appear in landscapes of both films and games that reference mystical plots, whereas action-adventure marketing images tend to highlight strong and aggressive male heroes, able to engage in conquest and rescue. These images objectify the community as one that is unable to determine its own fate and set it in a passive landscape, presented as exotic, which invites others to impose their scripts.

These maps, then, suggest boundaries, obscuring the textures within, that may be transgressed according to the whims and justifications of those able to do so. In this analysis, I considered whether these maps endure. The period of time considered in this study features the US concern with the threat of terror, accentuated by the events of 9/11 and informing subsequent military intervention. Since that time, many communities within the region have engaged in political protests, experienced government repression, and witnessed the rise of Daesh. Following 9/11, the United States targeted financial resources and engaged in military interventions in Iraq and Afghanistan, shifting away from the previous priorities of development assistance to Israel and Egypt, countries that have been rewarded for their political alliances with US leadership.

After 9/11, foreign aid to the region substantially increased over a decade, before a gradual decline. Similarly, news attention to the Middle East increased following this event for about half a decade, most frequently visible when US involvement was seen in heroic terms or violent actions offered justification for rescue.

Films referencing the Middle East increased along a trajectory that followed the rise of television news coverage of this region.

More specifically, news that was identified as focusing on violence increased along a similar rate as the rise of action-adventure films, particularly post-2010, a period also more likely to focus on contemporary rather than historical or mythical time periods. The link over time between violence in the news and conflict in films is worth further exploration.

US public agencies, television news, and popular culture contribute to a mapping of the Middle East that accentuates justifications for rescue and conquest. These justifications manifest in the narratives of action-adventure games and films, of development assistance, and of television news focusing on violence. US government decisions regarding when to intervene, as in Iraq, or not, as in Syria, become portrayed in ways that reinforce simplistic tropes. Narratives that highlight despair and incompetence, along with villainy and corruption, enable an entry for heroic intrusion.

The United States Narrating the Middle East

Through analyses of development programs, popular culture, and news texts, I identify prevalent themes across genres. The sentiment of despair feeds stories of violence in news reports, development initiatives, and rescue in popular culture. A rescue narrative prevails across these sources, positioning conflict as inevitable, thereby making rescue necessary.

The overriding genre featuring the Middle East in film, television, and interactive games, is action-adventure. Characters from the region, as well as from the global South, feature as victims and villains, requiring the intervention of more lightly shaded men from the global North. Gendered storylines differentiate vulnerability from venerability, while also distinguishing the independent and free women from the global North, who are able to drive and employ technologies, from the helpless women of the global South, who are barely surviving in antithetical conditions. This simplistic narrative resonates clearly with US development programs in the region, which is also approached through gendered frames and justifies assistance as necessary.

The violence that builds with suspense in action-adventure sequences also serves news narratives, which increase coverage of the Middle East at times of crisis, such as 9/11 in 2001 and the rise of Daesh in 2014, as well as times of projected victory, such as the execution of Saddam Hussein in 2006. In contrast to news in general, news specific to this region projects comparatively more anger and negativity, and it incorporates more religious references.

The rescue of people in an action-adventure narrative connects with another theme: empire adventure. Whereas in the former, the United States justifies its heroic intervention based on need, in the latter the acquisition of artifacts, land, or oil is based on an assertion of universal access and privileging of value over regional sovereignty. This sense of entitlement is enabled through envisioning communities as blank slates, unable to manage their own historical objects and art, natural resources, or commerce. As such, the Middle East serves as a setting for characters from outside the region to enact their stories. Indiana Jones, for example, has every right to seek and remove what he believes to have value, just as US government agencies and corporations position themselves as entitled to oil and other resources.

Though less prevalent than assertions of rescue and empire, another theme posits the Middle East as a magical kingdom, building on fantasy and avoiding historical context and contemporary politics. The tension inherent in this positioning becomes particularly strong in representations of Egypt, with mystical plots that feature pyramids and mummies, as opposed to the exposition of powerful political movements and repression in contemporary life. Representations in popular culture relying on magical kingdom narratives increased in post-9/11 film debuts, while comedies that feature some element of the region, already very few in previous years, have become nonexistent.

In the immediate years after 9/11, US military intervention, governmental development assistance, and news attention to the Middle East increased. Following suit, production and distribution of action-adventure films featuring the Middle East increased as well, contributing to an accentuation of rescue narratives. While this articulation has changed over time, what has endured is the strong and consistent empire adventure narrative. The only way for characters from the region to be featured as heroes is through the magical kingdom genre, but given the limitations of this framework, these heroes are limited in their contemporary relevance. Next, I review the consequences of these enduring and accelerating narratives.

The United States Mediating the Middle East

Relying on a theoretical foundation that privileges the contextual nature of mediating, I consider the consequences of these persistent and prevalent narratives. The architecture afforded through the *prism* framework allows us to connect the concerns raised through critical cultural studies with the implications of media reliance on dimensions of prejudice. Understanding the prisms created through practices of production, distribution, and interpretation position the optical refractions as social constructions with significant political foundations and implications. The projections of this prism highlight hostilities in US attitudes, particularly fear of immigrants, the threat of Islam, and projections of racism. This research confirms considerable scholarship that shows how these mediated prisms become particularly pronounced in shaping norms when people have little direct experience or familiarity with the issues or communities filtered through these media lenses.

The analyses presented in the preceding chapter confirm that concerns about the dominance of stereotypes in media are warranted. Given the prevalence of action-adventure as a central genre through which Middle East settings and characters are portrayed, the study's national survey focuses on the extent to which this affinity predicts prejudice within the United States toward the Middle East. It is crucial to recognize that experiences with hate crime in the United States are quite divergent between different communities: while only 15 percent of those of European descent had experience with hate crimes or knew someone who had, over half of all others did, whether Arab Americans, African Americans, or Latinx. This divergence serves as a central indicator of prejudice. Action-adventure fans with no hate crime experience, who did not identify as Arab American, posed the strongest level of prejudice against Arab and Muslim communities in the United States.

Fear of the Middle East was also clearly related to action-adventure affinity, which is significant given the dominantly problematic characterizations of the genre found in this research project and other studies. The hostility was most pronounced among male fans with little connection to the studied cultural identities. This evidence is significant but needs to be positioned within a more broadly conceptualized fear of terrorism in the world at large, also strongly connected to action-adventure experience. Given the methodological limitations of this survey, the correlations identified may indicate that those with dispositions that feel threatened by terrorism may enjoy action-adventure, which may then be reinforcing this sense of global threat and personal vulnerability.

The prism of fear integrates a more generalized concern with global terrorism and a perceived threat from the Middle East. In addition, prejudice against Muslim and Arab Americans is significantly related to fear of the Middle East. However, these internal prejudices are not correlated with fear of global terrorism, suggesting that these perceptions follow a spectrum of hostilities.

The research explored in this book engages crucial issues in US culture concerning Arab and Muslim American experience, as well as foreign policies and interventions. Concern with prejudice, however, extends to other communities that are particularly at risk given health concerns and hate crimes. Rhetoric from US leadership may reinforce prejudicial and hateful acts. In the next section, I consider the project ahead and suggest ways we might consider moving from current strictures toward more empathic and positive communication.

Moving Forward

The summary of this comprehensive project brings us to bleak conclusions. Simplistic narratives that accentuate differences prevail over time and across genres. The accumulated effects of these stereotypes inspire and reinforce prejudice, justifying public policies and resource allocations, while contributing to the rise in hate crimes and movements. In conclusion, I highlight ways that we might be able to shift these narratives, with collective and concerted effort, both in our personal lives and in our production of media.

In our personal lives, we can do more to encourage civility in our discourse and respect for diversity of opinion. In our social interactions and our educational programs, we can recognize that dialogue is essential. We do not want to promote civility that silences key voices, but rather a civility that encourages us to listen and to engage.

Within media industries, we can do more to supportive diversity of perspective in the creation and distribution of communication. Through our advocacy, we can raise concerns with existing media, contribute toward improved representations, and support more compassionate policies.

Through strategic communication intervention, we can educate our communities. Grounding the assumptions made in this research project, the Arab American Institute (2015), confirming Ogan et al. (2014), documents enduring and negative public attitudes toward Arab and Muslim Americans. Such attitudes are born of a lack of familiarity with or education about these communities. Although these perceptions may appear to be solidly entrenched among certain groups, they may be amenable to change through direct personal experience (Ahmed & Matthes, 2017) or through initiating strategic media literacy programs (Scharrer & Ramasubramanian, 2015; Tukachinsky et al., 2015). Strategic interventions may include support for direct cross-cultural experiences through travel and other programs, as well as through communication campaigns. Given that lack of familiarity or lack of experience creates a vulnerability to internalization of dominant narratives (e.g., AAI, 2015; Ahmed & Matthes, 2017), building programs to connect people directly across cultures is essential.

Strategic advocacy also has the potential for contribution and merits serious consideration, given the significance of the problem. Social and political movements can engage in political advocacy to mobilize protests and shift narratives, working toward enduring change. For example, discourse on the projected realism of *The Siege* was shifted, albeit slightly, when Arab American groups organized and protested the premiere of the film, illustrating that hegemonic narratives can be contested (Wilkins & Downing, 2002).

Given the documented potential for positive content to contribute toward more sympathetic perspectives and policies (Saleem et al., 2015), strategic communication is worth exploring through implementation and careful evaluation. Strategic entertainment-education television may reduce prejudice through viewer identification and vicarious connection with key characters (Murrar & Brauer, 2017; Slater & Rouner, 2002), which may then contribute toward sympathy with those in other communities (Ortiz & Harwood, 2007).

Interactivity in games may also expand perspectives, particularly if participants choose to play the role of terrorist and not just the hero (as in *Modern Warfare* 2, Schulzke, 2013) or if more diverse professionals work on the production of games. In contrast to the US Army's several editions of *America's Army*, exhibiting a strong patriotic perspective, Arab-produced video games offer more humanizing Arab roles (Šisler, 2008), with the potential to shift alliances (Alhabash & Wise, 2015). This scholarship offers justification for increasing diversity among media professionals in the production of content.

The more we can do to develop educational and outreach programs that create opportunities for students and citizens to engage in direct and sustained interaction across cultural and social boundaries, the more we can hope to inspire empathy and compassion. This guided and thoughtful direct contact should be our priority. It could take the form of study abroad or study away programs for students, as well as outreach projects requiring collaboration. In a time of collapsing study-abroad programs, we need to consider the diversity of communities as a way to promote these significant experiences. There are many ways to create interventions that promote empathy. While direct interaction warrants attention and support, another path calls for communication literacy, inspiring students to become critical agents able to analyze the credibility of popular culture, news, data, and other public discourse, and engage accordingly.

Communication Literacy

Critical analysis of media is key if we are to cultivate informed and questioning communities. By communication literacy, I intentionally encompass attention to critical media literacy, news literacy, and data literacy, toward a framework that implies our need to question public discourse more broadly, particularly given blurring genres and repeating narratives across policies, news, and fiction.

Critical media literacy highlights the importance of media texts repeating familiar patterns of representation, which then become internalized as strong social norms (Grossberg et al., 2006). This framework calls attention not just to media representations in texts, but also to the context of their production, particularly given political dynamics and economic structures. Luke and Sefton-Green (2018) connect critical media literacy with digital ethics, focusing on the implications of an increasingly digitized society. They remind us of the importance of situating these literacies within broader discussions of ideological contexts and a political economy of ownership and production. Key to this conceptualization is the foregrounding of critical analysis that moves beyond reflection at an individual level toward understanding the social and political dimensions that structure our production, distribution, and interpretation. Druick (2016) warns us against seeing media literacy as a simplistic approach that may normalize unquestioning celebrations of technologies and neoliberal discourse. This narrow approach to media literacy may end up legitimating an educational approach that serves techno-capitalism by producing a trained labor force and eager consumer base but not critical citizens.

Making communication literacy relevant to engaged citizenship is addressed in recent work concerning participatory democracy in an increasingly digital world. Recognizing a shift away from in-person townhall meetings toward collective digital discussions, increasingly pertinent in a time of global pandemic and local closures, Mihailidis and Thevenin (2013) focus on digital media literacy to build critical and creative competencies that allow people to be stronger agents of social change. Engaged citizenship requires an ability to think and act critically, particularly through prevalent digital and social media. Becoming more informed and engaged citizens also requires attention to active voice and listening.

Macnamara (2013) elaborates on the importance of listening as a necessary complement of voice, conceptualizing audiences as fragmented across media platforms but able to be educated into an "architecture of listening" that gives recognition and response to voices in a media environment, attending to "appropriate policies, structures, resources and facilities" (p. 168). He reminds us of Couldry's (2010) articulation of voice requiring both audience and listening, suggesting that approaches to media literacy should be predicated on the importance of voice within these actively engaged processes. Given the prevalence of voice as mediated in contemporary culture, communication scholars have studied the effectiveness of media literacy interventions.

Integrating these particular concepts into a more comprehensive framework, I propose communication literacy as a conceptual architecture uniting production with reception, agnostic as to whether relying on digital or other platforms, or whether considering nonfiction versus fiction. The blurring of genre boundaries, increasingly intersected screens with tactile contact, and an overly saturated world of cascading and compelling information, allows us an overarching framework in which to move past simplistic areas of focus and to include additional dimensions such as data, visual, and numerical literacies as well. Cairo (2019) joins others, such as Lewis, McAdams, and Stalph (2020), reminding us that visual representations of data require an ability to read and critique. Data literacy then becomes an important component of this educational program toward an ethics of presentation and transparency.

While much of this work focuses on analysis of texts, to highlight the representations that privilege and disparage our communities, I advocate for a critical approach to communication literacy that positions analyses of texts within contexts of their production as well as distribution and interpretation. Moreover, this critical analysis needs to be connected with civic engagement, to encourage responsible and ethical social action.

Media Literacy Intervention

Media literacy educational programs are not new, though our design and implementation of these projects may need to adapt to changing conditions and in response to informative evaluations. A significant meta-analysis of over fifty intervention studies published before 2009 offers some valuable findings concerning the overall positive effect of media literacy interventions. Jeong et al. (2012) find that across these studies, media literacy programs do well in creating critical awareness and skills, thus demoting beliefs in media realism, promoting self-efficacy, and reducing problematic behaviors. However, these programs were somewhat less effective in shifting broader social norms. Most relevant to the research project in this book is attention to critical analysis, which appears to be enabled through these strategic interventions. Given that norms are more broadly conceptualized and enduring than specific attitudes, finding less of an effect on the former may be a product of more immediate testing prevalent in published research, rather than anticipating trends over longer periods of time.

To review the potential for communication literacy education, I consider the extent to which media, news, and other literacy interventions are able to impact knowledge and skills, perceptions and norms, and motivations toward engagement and other behaviors. Some of these interventions are directed toward high school students and others have been tested with college courses across a variety of cultural settings. Given a convincing literature of communication campaigns, along with the meta-analysis cited above, we expect there to be a stronger propensity to increase skills and expertise, followed by the ability to shift attitudes, and then by intentional or reported behaviors. But civic engagement is considered to be more than a targeted behavior for individuals, as it integrates participatory and critical pedagogy as well as attention to dialogic approaches to citizens in enacted and collective change.

Contribution of Communication Literacy Intervention to Knowledge and Skills

Scholarship investigating the existing knowledge and concerns of younger adults identifies areas for education, given increasingly networked and digital consumption of news among this group. A survey of Australian youth (Notley & Dezuanni, 2019) finds that although this cohort may be heavily consuming digital news and concerned with the threat of fake news, they do not feel confident of their abilities to discern credibility, and rarely check the news sources they do not trust. Toepfl (2014) concludes from interviewing Russian youth that this group also needs education to assess political news through digital sources, including analysis of messages and the role of media in society. These studies, then, support a need for communication literacy programs in high schools and universities.

Research attention to knowledge and skills tends to focus on news literacy programs designed to enhance critical analysis of authenticity, credibility, and realism. Martens and Hobbs (2015) assessed the effectiveness of media literacy education with high school students in the United States, demonstrating that participation in these programs improved expertise about media institutions and the effects of their reportage, and provided skills to analyze messages. Analysis skills contribute to assessment of authenticity and credibility of sources and stories. Shen and colleagues (2018) relied on experimental procedures to determine that assessment of image authenticity in online presentations is predicated on experience and expertise with digital media, suggesting that education concerning digital imaging should strengthen abilities to ascertain image authenticity. These studies support more comprehensive literature demonstrating the potential of educational programs in building expertise.

Contribution of Communication Literacy Intervention to Perceptions and Norms

While studies of media literacy programs' ability to strengthen analytical skills tend to focus on news, research focusing on attitudinal shifts include both news and popular culture as subjects of inquiry. When considering news literacy, researchers explore implications for political attitudes, such as perceptions of participatory governance and fear of terrorism. Through a panel study of university students in the United States, Tully and Vraga (2018) find that those who appreciate critical thinking and those who are more politically partisan are more likely to aspire to news media literacy. Also, those who then perceive themselves as media literate are more likely to engage with information with which they disagree. This sense of self-confidence and competence, then, may be a critical dimension in communication literacy intervention.

Fear of terrorism has direct relevance to the research presented in this book, not only because news coverage is likely to increase perceived threat, but also because strategic media literacy education may have the potential to mitigate this fear. Bergan and Lee (2018) study the latter link, building on classic cultivation theory specifying correlations between media consumption and attitudes toward a "mean world," resonant with the findings presented in the previous chapter. Contrary to prevalent scholarship indicating a link between literacy intervention and ability to assess credibility and authenticity, Bergan and Lee's study, dividing groups into those reading news of terrorism and those reading less sensational news, demonstrate media literacy as failing to reduce fear of terrorism. Although their research did not result in significant findings, there are enough caveats to warrant further investigation: the subject of terrorism selected for their study concerned an actual and recent bombing in Boston; and assessing the credibility of a source may engage different processes, depending on type and source of story. Given a more comprehensive sense of threat with our current global pandemic, we need to explore the potential for strategic communication to enhance analytic skills in a variety of domains.

Communication literacy needs to address more than news; it must also integrate critical attention to popular culture and advertising. Some studies have begun to consider how strategic education may encourage critical analysis relevant to representations of gender, race, ethnicity, and other identities. Sekarasih and colleagues (2018) build on a careful panel study of middle-school students in the United States, contrasting their attitudes prior to and following a media literacy education program focused on advertising. Following this intervention, students increasingly disliked advertisements, particularly those that lacked realism. Female students were increasingly critical of gendered portrayals and violent images, particularly when compared with their male counterparts.

Other research considers the potential for strategic education to reduce prejudice. In their overview of literature, Scharrer and Ramasubramanian (2015) conclude that media literacy works best when including analyses of messages and comparisons with other media examples. Based on their review, they believe that media literacy education may be able to promote multicultural understanding and reduce racial and ethnic stereotypes, particularly with longer and sustained educational programs. Through a quasi-experiment with college students in the United States, Erba et al.

(2019) confirm the potential for media literacy intervention to produce favorable attitudes toward minority communities, though the effects of the education decreased over time. They also raise an important point, in that single educational programs still work against a media landscape saturated with racial stereotypes. They join other scholars, such as Bhatia and Patkhak-Shelat (2017) concerning religious stereotypes in Indian media, proposing to use media literacy to create more sympathetic attitudes toward various and diverse communities.

Resonant with the particular subject of this research project, Hobbs and colleagues (2011) assessed US elementary student perceptions of the Middle East in order to create proposals for media literacy programs to reduce stereotypes. The film *Aladdin* served as an important illustration of the kinds of problematic representations easily available to this group. Again, given the prevalence of these kinds of images and narratives, established in this research as well as through other scholarship, literacy education addresses a challenging but critical concern.

Contribution of Communication Literacy Intervention to Individual Behavior and Civic Engagement

Media literacy interventions have been shown to be effective for increasing knowledge and, in some instances, inducing attitudinal changes more favorable to various communities stereotyped in media and, among some groups, more critical of mediated messages. Communication campaign research in a variety of domains demonstrates the tendency for the effects of knowledge, attitudes, and behaviors to change proportionately in hierarchical descent, following more psychological traditions of analyzing individual-level outcomes. The question of whether literacy interventions have the potential to create motivations or behavior changes is worth asking, although more dominant methodological approaches limit analyses to immediate rather than enduring change.

Through a meta-analysis of media literacy focusing on health behaviors, Xie et al. (2019) determine a moderate effect on changing actions such as smoking, drinking, and eating habits. In another review, Bulger and Davison (2018) expand scrutiny of media literacy programs to include other aspects, such as teacher training and parental support, toward their conclusion that behaviors may be susceptible to change in some instances but that we need a better understanding of the broader context of mediated messages and cultural climate.

It is worth differentiating literacy interventions that appear to serve an economic status quo rather than question inequity in economic conditions. For example, Suwana (2017) describes an empowering literacy program in Indonesia designed to increase women's digital media skills, while recognizing that an overarching patriarchal ideology limits its potential for more significant impact. Development communication research raises similar critiques of empowerment programs (Wilkins, 2016) that implicitly support integration into capitalist economies, reinforcing neoliberal ideologies rather than promoting critical perspectives that question programs that accentuate inequities.

Civic engagement offers one significant potential path to action that may be motivated through strategic communication intervention. Critical media literacy particularly, focusing on the relationship between popular culture and cultural industries, aims to promote critical consciousness as well as civic engagement (Leurs et al., 2018). Based on their study of high school students in the United States, Martens and Hobbs (2015) believe that media literacy has the potential to promote intellectual curiosity and self-efficacy, which then enable civic engagement.

This focus on critical literacy inspires educational programs that improve our ability to engage in democratic social change. Some of these programs envision attention to production as a necessary complement to analysis of texts and a way of enabling participation. In their study of teens in the Netherlands, Leurs and colleagues (2018) rely on ethnographic data from migrant youth to suggest that critical media literacy education produces more confidence in abilities to self-represent in creating videos and writing narratives. They believe that production skills and confidence will lead to political participation.

Relying on the Association for Education in Journalism and Mass Communication (AEJMC) as a resource, Ashley (2015) considers this issue comprehensively, questioning how communication and journalism instructors integrate media literacy into their courses. Most instructors do see their goal as working to enable students to engage with media, to respect diverse perspectives, and to promote civic engagement. Most of these courses, though, lack the critical media perspective prescribed in this conclusion, relying more on skills and training than on situating analysis with attention to cultural, political, and economic contexts.

In contrast, to address dominant and enduring narratives grounded in problematic mapping of communities and territories, I advocate for an educational approach that builds on critical pedagogy, enabling participatory and engaged strategies. An emerging dialogue connecting critical pedagogy with social justice should motivate and inform our educational policies and projects

(Chen & Lawless, 2019; Kahlenberg, 2019; Mora, 2016). Our hope for critical communication literacy relies on what we are able to do through our educational practice and our social critique.

Shifting the Prism

This research project confirms concerns raised with dominant US articulations of the Middle East. Current prisms of prejudice can shift toward more constructive and respectful communication. I propose communication literacy as one mode of strategic intervention, but for this to work as an effective and sustained project, we also need to support changes in our media industries, public policies, and advocacy programs. This is a matter of employing ethics and empathy, through collective and intentional strategies, to create stronger and more supportive communication.

Notes

Chapter 2. Mapping the Middle East

1. This agency includes the following territories in western Asia: Bahrain, Egypt, Iraq, Jordan, Kuwait, Lebanon, Libya, Morocco, Oman, Palestine, Qatar, Saudi Arabia, the Sudan, the Syrian Arab Republic, Tunisia, the United Arab Amirates, and Yemen.

2. Personal communication with Joe Straubhaar, January 3, 2019.

3. Personal communication with Wenhong Chen, January 3, 2019.

4. Personal communication with John Downing, January 3, 2019.

5. Afghanistan, Algeria, Armenia, Azerbaijan, Bahrain, Cyprus, Egypt, Georgia, Iran, Iraq, Jordan, Kazakhstan, Kuwait, Kyrgyzstan, Lebanon, Libya, Morocco, Oman, Palestinian National Authority, Qatar, Saudi Arabia, Syria, Tunisia, Turkey, Turkmenistan, United Arab Emirates, Uzbekistan, Yemen. Library of Congress, https://www.loc.gov/rr/amed/nes/neshome.html, https://www.loc.gov/rr/main/religion/ne.html, accessed March 2021.

6. US Government Bookstore, https://bookstore.gpo.gov/catalog/international-foreign-affairs/middle-east (italics mine), accessed February 22, 2019.

7. US Embassy, https://www.us-consulate.net/category/middle-east, https://www.us-consulate.net/category/africa, accessed February 22, 2019.

8. US Department of State, Bureau of Near Eastern Affairs, http://www.state.gov/p/nea/, accessed February 22, 2019.

9. Central Intelligence Agency, Central Intelligence Agency, https://www.cia.gov/the-world-factbook/, accessed March 7, 2021.

10. FBI, https://www.fbi.gov/contact-us/legal-attache-offices/middle-east, accessed July 2, 2019.

11. USAID, https://www.usaid.gov/where-we-work/middle-east. https://www.usaid.gov/where-we-work/middle-east, accessed February 22, 2019.

12. US Department of Agriculture, Foreign Agricultural Service, .http://www.fas.usda.gov/regions, accessed February 22, 2019.

13. USAID, https://www.usaid.gov/where-we-work/middle-east includes Egypt, Iraq, Jordan, Lebanon, Libya, Morocco, Syria, Tunisia, West Bank and Gaza, Yemen, Middle East Regional, and Regional Cooperation Program (MERC), accessed June 3, 2019.

14. USAID, https://www.usaid.gov/where-we-work/middle-east/merc, accessed June 3, 2019.

15. US–Middle East Partnership Initiative, http://mepi.state.gov/index.html, accessed February 22, 2019.

16. These are not mutually exclusive, often appearing in the same news item.

17. USAID, https://www.usaid.gov/where-we-work/middle-east, accessed June 30, 2018.

Chapter 4. Mediating the Middle East

This chapter was previously published as "US Prisms and Prejudice through Mediating the Middle East," *International Communication Gazette* 82, no. 6 (2020), 526–544. doi:10.1177/1748048519853752.

1. Noting that these categories are blurred rather than distinct, given connections between Arab heritage and situated ancestry as Caucasian, these categories allowed respondents to choose which identity felt most prominent for themselves within US culture.

References

Afshar, H. (2013). The Politics of Fear: What Does It Mean to Those Who Are Otherized and Feared? *Ethnic and Racial Studies*, 36(1), 9–27. doi:10.1080/01419870.2013.738821.

Aguayo, M. (2009). Representations of Muslim Bodies in the Kingdom: Deconstructing Discourses in Hollywood. *Global Media Journal*, 2(2), 41–56.

Ahmed, S., & Matthes, J. (2017). Media Representation of Muslims and Islam from 2000 to 2015: A Meta-analysis. *The International Communication Gazette*, 79(3), 219–244. https://doi.org/10.1177/1748048516656305.

Akram, S. M. (2002). The Aftermath of September 11, 2001: The Targeting of Arabs and Muslims in America. *Arab Studies Quarterly*, 24(2–3), 61–118.

Albdour, M., Lewin, L., Kavanaugh, K., Hong, J. S., & Wilson, F. (2017). Arab American Adolescents' Perceived Stress and Bullying Experiences: A Qualitative Study. *Western Journal of Nursing Research*, 39(12), 1567–1588.

Alhabash, S., & Wise, K. (2015). Playing Their Game: Changing Stereotypes of Palestinians and Israelis through Videogame Play. *New Media and Society*, 17(8), 1358–1376.

Alsultany, E. (2012). Protesting Muslim Americans as Patriotic Americans: The All-American Muslim Controversy. *Journal of Mass Media Ethics*, 27(2), 145–148. https://doi.org/10.1080/08900523.2012.684588.

———. (2015). The Cultural Politics of Islam in US Reality Television. *Communication, Culture & Critique*, 9(4), 595–613. doi:10.1111/cccr.1212.

———. (2016). Representations of Arabs, Muslims, and Iranians in an Era of Complex Characters and Story Lines. *Film Criticism*, 40(1). doi: http://dx.doi.org/10.3998/fc.13761232.0040.102.

Altheide, D. L. (2013). Media Logic, Social Control, and Fear. *Communication Theory*, 23, 223–238. https://doi.org/10.1111/comt.12017.

Alvarez, A. (2015). *IBIS World Industry Report N003: Video Games in the US*. IBS World, June. http://clients1.ibisworld.com/reports/us/industry/default.aspx?entid=2003. Accessed June 3, 2016.

Al-Zo'by, M. (2015). Representing Islam in the Age of Neo-orientalism: Media, Politics and Identity. *Journal of Arab & Muslim Media Research*, 8(3), 217–238. doi: 10.1386/jammr.8.3.217_1.

American-Arab Anti-Discrimination Committee (ADC). (2008). *2003–2007 Report on Hate Crimes and Discrimination against Arab Americans*. https://www.issuelab.org/resource/2003-2007-report-on-hate-crimes-and-discrimination-against-arab-americans.html. Accessed October 3, 2017.

———. (2017). *The MENA Category and Looking Ahead*. ADC Convention Panel, September 12. http://www.adc.org/2017/09/adc-convention-panel-census-2020-the-mena-category-and-looking-ahead/. Accessed September 14, 2017.

Amin-Khan, T. (2012). New Orientalism, Securitisation and the Western Media's Incendiary Racism. *Third World Quarterly*, 33(9), 1595–1610. doi:10.1080/01436597.2012.720831.

Anaz, N., & Purcell, D. (2010). Geopolitics of Film: Valley of the Wolves: Iraq and Its Reception in Turkey and Beyond. *The Arab World Geographer*, 13(1), 34–49.

Arab American Institute (AAI). (2015). *American Attitudes toward Arabs and Muslims*. http://www.aaiusa.org/american_attitudes_toward_ arabs_and_muslims_2015. Accessed December 15, 2017.

———. (2017a). Demographics. http://www.aaiusa.org/demographics. Accessed September 29, 2017.

———. (2017b). AAI Issue Brief: Hate Crimes. https://d3n8a8pro7vhmx.cloudfront.net/aai/pages/12067/attachments/original/1493399028/HATE_CRIMES_ISSUE_BRIEF_2017_NO_LOGOS.pdf?1493399028. Accessed October 3, 2017.

Ashley, S. (2015). Media Literacy in Action? What Are We Teaching in Introductory College Media Studies Courses? *Journalism & Mass Communication Educator*, 70(2), 161–173. https://doi.org/10.1177/1077695815572191.

Bateson, G. (1972). *Steps to an Ecology of Mind.* Chicago: University of Chicago Press.

Baum, M. (2002). Sex, Lies, and War: How Soft News Brings Foreign Policy to the Inattentive Public. *American Political Science Review*, 96(1). 91–109. doi: https://doi.org/10.1017/S0003055402004252.

Bayraktaroğlu, K. (2014). The Muslim Male Character Typology in American Cinema Post–9/11. *Digest of Middle East Studies*, 23(2), 345–359. https://doi .org/10.1111/dome.12054.

BBC. (2019). BBC World Service. The 1930s. http://www.bbc.co.uk/world service/history/story/2007/02/070123_html_1930s.shtml. Accessed July 17, 2019.

Bell, G. C. (2017). *Talking Black and White: An Intercultural Exploration of Twenty-First-Century Racism, Prejudice, and Perception.* Lanham. MD: Rowman & Littlefield.

Benjamin, D., & Simon, S. (2019). America's Great Satan: The 40-Year Obsession with Iran. *Foreign Affairs*, 98(6), 56–66.

Bergan, D., & Lee, H. (2018). Media Literacy and Response to Terror News. *Journal of Media Literacy Education*, 10(3), 43–56. https://doi.org/10.23860 /JMLE-2018-10-03-03.

Beydoun, K. A. (2018). *American Islamophobia: Understanding the Roots and Rise of Fear.* Oakland: University of California Press.

Bhatia, K. V., & Pathak-Shelat, M. (2017). Media Literacy as a Pathway to Religious Literacy in Pluralistic Democracies: Designing a Critical Media Education Pedagogy for Primary School Children in India. *Interactions: Studies in Communication & Culture*, 8(2–3), 189–209. https://doi.org/10 .1386/iscc.8.2-3.189_1.

The Bridge Initiative. (2017). Two Decades of Prejudice: Hate Crimes against U.S. Muslims since 1996. Georgetown University Bridge Initiative. http:// bridge.georgetown.edu/infographic/two-decades-of-prejudice-fbi-hate -crime-statistics/. Accessed October 3, 2017.

Brown, M. (2019). British Museum to Return Heads Looted in Afghan War. *The Guardian*, July 8. https://www.theguardian.com/culture/2019/jul /08/british-museum-return-looted-afghan-artefacts-found-heathrow. Accessed July 25, 2019.

Bulger, M., & Davison, P. (2018). The promises, challenges and futures of media literacy. *Journal of Media Literacy Education*, 10(1), 1–21.

Busselle, R., & Bilandzic, H. (2008). Fictionality and Perceived Realism in Experiencing Stories: A Model of Narrative Comprehension and Engagement. *Communication Theory*, 18, 255–280. doi:10.1111/ j.1468-2885.2008 .00322.

Cairo, A. (2019). *How Charts Lie: Getting Smarter about Visual Communication.* New York: W.W. Norton & Company.

Castonguay, J. (2015). Fictions of Terror: Complexity, Complicity and Insecurity in *Homeland*. *Cinema Journal*, 54(4), 139–145. doi: 10.1353/cj.2015 .0045.

Chalcraft, J. (2016). *Popular Politics: In the Making of the Modern Middle East.* Cambridge: Cambridge University Press.

Chen, Y. W., & Lawless, B. (2019). Teaching Critical Moments within Neoliberal Universities: Exploring Intercultural Communication Pedagogy. *Journal of Intercultural Communication Research*, 48(1): 5, 553573. doi: 10.1080/17475759.2019.1683056.

Chomsky, N. (2016). *Who Rules the World?* New York: Henry Holt and Company.

Christensen, C. L., & Peterson, L. N. (2017). Introduction: Being Old in the Age of Mediatization. *Nordicom Review*, 38, 3–7. https://doi.org/10.1515 /nor-2017-0399.

Cloud, D. (2004). To Veil the Threat of Terror: Afghan Women and the 'Clash of Civilizations' in the Imagery of the U.S. War on Terrorism. *Quarterly Journal of Speech*, 90(3), 285–306.

Cole, J. (2015). *The New Arabs: How the Millennial Generation Is Changing the Middle East.* New York: Simon & Schuster.

Colle, R. D. (1989). Communicating Scientific Knowledge. In J. L. Compton (Ed.), *The Transformation of International Agricultural Research and Development*. Boulder: Lynne Rienner.

Cooper, A. F. (2008). *Celebrity Diplomacy.* Boulder: Paradigm.

Couldry, N. (2008). Mediatization or Mediation? Alternative Understandings of the Emergent Space of Digital Storytelling. *New Media & Society*, 10(3), 373–391.

——. (2010). *Why Voice Matters: Culture and Politics after Neoliberalism*. Los Angeles: Sage Publications.
——. (2012). *Media, Society, World: Social Theory and Digital Media Practice*. Cambridge, UK: Polity Press.
Couldry, N., & Hepp, A. (2013). Conceptualizing Mediatization: Contexts, Traditions, Arguments. *Communication Theory*, 23(3), 191–202.
——. (2017). *The Mediated Construction of Reality*. Cambridge, UK: Polity Press.
Crane, D. (2014). Cultural Globalization and the Dominance of the American Film Industry: Cultural Policies, National Film Industries, and Transnational Film. *International Journal of Cultural Policy*, 20(4), 365–382. https://doi.org/10.1080/10286632.2013.832233.
Culcasi, K. (2010). Constructing and Naturalizing the Middle East. *Geographical Review*, 100(4), 583–597.
Curti, G. H. (2011). The Middle of Where? Media Geography and the Middle East. *Aether*, 8, 1–15.
Davison, R. H. (1960). Where Is the Middle East? *Foreign Affairs*, 38(4), 665–675.
Dawson, A. (2016). Drone Executions, Urban Surveillance, and the Imperial Gaze. In A. Lubin & M. Kraidy (Eds.), *American Studies Encounters the Middle East* (pp. 241–262). Chapel Hill: University of North Carolina Press. http://www.jstor.org/stable/10.5149/9781469628851_lubin.13. Accessed March 29, 2021.
Dittmer, J. (2005). Captain America's Empire: Reflections on Identity, Popular Culture, and Post-9/11 Geopolitics. *Annals of the Association of American Geographers*, 95(3), 626–-643. https://doi.org/10.1111/j.1467-8306.2005.00478.x.
Doran, M. S. (2019). The Dream Palace of the Americans: Why Ceding Land Will Not Bring Peace. *Foreign Affairs*, 98(6), 21–29.
Downing, J. (2007). The Imperiled "American": Visual Culture, Nationality and US Foreign Policy. *International Journal of Communication*, 1(1), 24. http://ijoc.org/index.php/ijoc/article/view/111.
——. (2013). "Geopolitics" and "the Popular": An exploration. *Popular Communication*, 11, 7–16. https://doi.org/10.1080/15405702.2013.747939.

Downing, J., & Husband, C. (2005). *Representing Race*. London: Sage. http://dx.doi.org/10.4135/9781446220412.

Druick, Z. (2016). The Myth of Media Literacy. *International Journal of Communication*, 10, 1125–1144.

Dutta, M. J. (2011). *Communicating Social Change: Structure, Culture, and Agency*. New York: Routledge.

The Economist (2011). All the World's a Game. *Economist*. December 10.

Ekman, M. (2015). Online Islamophobia and the Politics of Fear: Manufacturing the Green Scare. *Ethnic and Racial Studies*, 38(11), 1986–2002. doi:10.1080/01419870.2015.1021264.

El-Nawawy, M., & Elmasry, M. H. (2017). Valuing Victims: A Comparative Framing Analysis of *The Washington Post's* Coverage of Violent Attacks against Muslims and Non-Muslims. *International Journal of Communication* 11, 1795–1815. doi:1932–8036/20170005.

Enghel, F. (2016). Understanding the Donor-Driven Practice of Development Communication: From Media Engagement to a Politics of Mediation. *Global Media Journal—Canadian Edition*. 9(1), 5–21.

Ehrenreich, B. (2009). *Bright-Sided: How the Relentless Promotion of Positive Thinking Has Undermined America*. New York: Metropolitan Books.

Erba, J., Chen, Y., & Kang, M. H. (2019). Using Media Literacy to Counter Stereotypical Images of Blacks and Latinos at a Predominantly White University. *Howard Journal of Communication*, 30(1), 1–22. https://doi.org/10.1080/10646175.2018.1423652.

Escobar, A. (1995). *Encountering Development: The Making and Unmaking of the Third World*. Princeton: Princeton University Press.

Evans, M. (2010). Framing International Conflicts: Media Coverage of Fighting in the Middle East. *International Journal of Media and Cultural Politics*, 6(2), 209–233. doi:10.1386/mcp.6.2.209_1.

Feuerherd, Ben. July 3, 2019. Rami Malek Gave Ultimatum Before Agreeing to Play 'Bond' Villain, *Page Six*. https://pagesix.com/2019/07/03/rami-malek-gave-ultimatum-before-agreeing-to-play-bond-villain/. Accessed July 7, 2019.

Fleck, R. K., & Kilby, C. (2010). Changing Aid Regimes? U.S. Foreign Aid from the Cold War to the War on Terror. *Journal of Development Economics*, 91, 185–197.

Foreign Affairs. (2019). Trump's Middle East. November/ December 2019. 98(6).

Gelt, J. (2019). Riz Ahmed Was Headed to a 'Star Wars' Event—until Homeland Security Stopped Him, *Los Angeles Times*, June 29. https://www.latimes.com/entertainment/la-et-mn-riz-ahmed-homeland-security-20190629-story.html. Accessed July 5, 2019.

Ghobrial, B., & Wilkins, K. (2015). The Politics of Political Communication: Competing News Discourses of the 2011 Egyptian News Protests. *International Communication Gazette*. doi: http://gaz.sagepub.com/content/77/2/129.

Gilroy, P. (2012). 'My Britain Is Fuck All' Zombie Multiculturalism and the Race Politics of Citizenship. *Identities: Global Studies in Culture and Power*, 19(4), 380–397. https://doi.org/10.1080/1070289X.2012.725512.

Grossberg, L., Wartella, E., Whitney, D., & Wise, J. (2006). *Media Making: Mass Media in a Popular Culture*, 2nd ed. London: Sage Publications.

Hatton, A. T., & Nielsen, M. E. (2016). "War on Terror" in Our Backyard: Effects of Framing and Violent ISIS Propaganda on Anti-Muslim Prejudice. *Behavioral Sciences of Terrorism and Political Aggression*, 8(3), 163–176. https://doi.org/10.1080/19434472.2015.1126341.

Hepp, A. (2019). *Deep Mediatization*. London: Routledge.

Hepp, A., Hjarvard, S., & Lundby, K. (2015). Mediatization: Theorizing the Interplay between Media, Culture and Society. *Media, Culture & Society*, 37(2), 314–324. https://doi.org/10.1177/0163443715573835.

Hjarvard, S. (2013). *The Mediatization of Culture and Society*. London, UK: Routledge.

Hobbs, R., Cabral, N., Ebrahimi, A., Yoon, J., & Al-Humaidan, R., (2011). Field-Based Teacher Education in Elementary Media Literacy as a Means to Promote Global Understanding. *Action in Teacher Education*, 33(2), 144–156. https://doi.org/10.1080/01626620.2011.569313.

Hooper, I. (2018). *Report: Anti-Muslim Bias Incidents, Hate Crimes Spike in Second Quarter of 2018*. Washington, DC: CAIR. https://www.cair.com/cair_report_anti_muslim_bias_incidents_hate_crimes_spike_in_second_quarter_of_2018.

Horsti, K. (2017). Digital Islamophobia: The Swedish Woman as a Figure of Pure and Dangerous Whiteness. *New Media & Society*, 19(9), 1440–1457. https://doi.org/10.1177/1461444816642169.

Ibrahim, D. (2010). The Framing of Islam on Network News Following the September 11th Attacks. *The International Communication Gazette*, 72(1), 111–125. https://doi.org/10.1177/1748048509350342.

Indyk, M. (2019). Disaster in the Desert: Why Trump's Middle East Plan Can't Work. *Foreign Affairs*, 98(6), 10–20.

Jeong, S., Cho, H., & Hwang, Y. (2012). Media Literacy Interventions: A Meta-analytic Review. *Journal of Communication*, 62(3), 454–472. https://doi.org/10.1111/j.1460-2466.2012.01643.x.

Johnson, K. R., & Loscocco, K. (2015). Black Marriage through the Prism of Gender, Race, and Class. *Journal of Black Studies*, 46(2), 142–171. https://doi.org/10.1177/0021934714562644.

Juneau, T. (2014). U.S. Power in the Middle East: Not Declining. *Middle East Policy*, 21 (2), 40–52.

Kahlenberg, S. (2019). Fusing Social Justice with Social Scientific Perspectives to Teach Content Analysis in Media Theory and Methods, *Communication Teacher*, 33(4), 292–297. doi: 10.1080/17404622.2019.1575438.

Kaler, A. (2010). Gender-as-Knowledge and AIDS in Africa: A Cautionary Tale. *Qualitative Sociology*, 33, 23–36. doi: 10.1007/s11133-009-9140-6.

Kapoor, I. (2013). *Celebrity Humanitarianism: The Ideology of Global Charity*. New York: Routledge.

Kohut, A., Doherty, A., Dimock, M., & Keeter, S. (2010). *Americans Spending More Time Following the News*. Pew Research Center. September 12. https://core.ac.uk/download/pdf/30682252.pdf. Accessed February 2, 2020.

Koppes, C. R. (1976). Captain Mahan, General Gordon, and the Origins of the Term 'Middle East,' *Middle Eastern Studies*, 12(1), 95–98. doi: 10.1080/00263207608700307.

Kozlovic, A. K. (2007). Islam, Muslims and Arabs in the Popular Hollywood Cinema. *Comparative Islamic Studies*, 3(2). doi: 10.1558/cis/v3i2.213.

Krieg, A. 2016. Externalizing the Burden of War: The Obama Doctrine and US Foreign Policy in the Middle East. *International Affairs*, 92(1), 97–113. https://doi.org/10.1111/1468-2346.12506.

Kumar, D. (2014). Mediating Racism: The New McCarthyites and the Matrix of Islamophobia. *Middle East Journal of Culture and Communication*, 7, 9–26. doi: 10.1163/18739865-00701001.

Kunelius, R., & Reunanen, E. (2016). The Changing Power of Journalism: The Two Phases of Mediatization. *Communication Theory*, 26(4), 369–388. doi: 10.1111/comt.12098.
Kurzman, C. (2018). *The Missing Martyrs: Why Are There So Few Muslim Terrorists?* 2nd ed. New York: Oxford University Press.
Lerner, D. (1958). *The Passing of Traditional Society: Modernizing the Middle East.* Glencoe: Free Press.
Leurs, K., Omerovic, E., Bruinenberg, H., & Sprenger, S. (2018). Critical Media Literacy through Making Media: A Key to Participation for Young Migrants? *Communications*, 43(3), 427–450. https://doi.org/10.1515/commun-2018-0017.
Lewis, N. P., McAdams, M., & Stalph, F. (2020). Data Journalism. *Journalism & Mass Communication Educator*, 75(1), 16–21. https://doi.org/10.1177/1077695820904971.
Li, T. M. (2007). *The Will to Improve: Governmentality, Development, and the Practice of Politics.* Durham: Duke University Press.
Livingston, S., & Lunt, P. (2014). *Mediatization: An Emerging Paradigm for Media and Communication Studies.* In K. Lundby (Ed.), *Mediatization of Communication*. Handbooks of Communication Science (pp. 703–724). Berlin: De Gruyter Mouton.
Lubin, A., & Kraidy, M. (Eds.). (2016). *American Studies Encounters the Middle East.* Chapel Hill: University of North Carolina Press.
Luke, A., & Sefton-Green, J. (2018). Critical Media Literacy and Digital Ethics. *Media Development*, 4, 6–13.
Lynch, M. (2007). *Voices of the New Arab Public: Iraq, Al Jazeera, and Middle East Politics Today.* New York: Columbia University Press.
Macnamara, J. (2013). Beyond Voice: Audience-Making and the Work and Architecture of Listening as New Media Literacies. *Continuum: Journal of Media & Cultural Studies*, 27(1), 160–175. https://doi.org/10.1080/10304312.2013.736950.
Makdisi, U. (2016). The Privilege of Acting upon Others: The Middle Eastern Exception to Anti-Exceptionalist Histories of the US and the World. In F. Costiglioa & M. J. Hogan (Eds.), *Explaining the History of American Foreign Relations* (pp. 203–216). Cambridge: Cambridge University Press.

Malley, R. (2019). The Unwanted Wars: Why the Middle East Is More Combustible Than Ever. *Foreign Affairs*, 98(6), 38–46.

Marchetti, G. (1989). Action-Adventure as Ideology. In I. Angus & S. Jhally (Eds.), *Cultural Politics in Contemporary America* (pp. 182–97). New York: Routledge.

Martens, H., & Hobbs, R. (2015). How Media Literacy Supports Civic Engagement in a Digital Age. *Atlantic Journal of Communication*, 23(2), 120–137. https://doi.org/10.1080/15456870.2014.961636.

Martin-Barbero., M. J. (1993). *Communication, Culture and Hegemony*. London: Sage.

Marzano, A. (2011). Reading the Israeli-Palestinian Conflict through an Islamophobic Prism: The Italian Press and the Gaza War. *Journal of Arab & Muslim Media Research*, 4(1), 63–78. https://doi.org/10.1386/jammr.4.1.63_1.

McAlister, M. (2005). *Epic Encounters: Culture, Media, and the U.S. Interests in the Middle East since 1945*. Updated edition. Berkeley: University of California Press.

McDonald, D. G. (2014). Narrative Research in Communication: Key Principles and Issues. *Review of Communication* 2(1), 115–132. doi: 10.12840/issn.2255-4165.2014.02.01.005.

McKee, R. (1997). *Story: Substance, Structure, Style, and the Principles of Screenwriting*. New York: Regan Books.

Mihailidis, P., & Thevenin, B. (2013). Media Literacy as a Core Competency for Engaged Citizenship in Participatory Democracy. *American Behavioral Scientist*, 57(11), 1611–1622. https://doi.org/10.1177/0002764213489015.

Mora, J. (2016). Socially Constructing Learning Space: Communication Theory and Pedagogy for Social Justice. *Review of Communication*, 16(2–3), 176–191. doi: 10.1080/15358593/2016.1187455.

Morey, P. (2010). Terrorvision. *Interventions*, 12(2), 215–264. https://doi.org/10.1080/1369801X.2010.489699.

Morey, P., & Yaqin, A. (2010). Muslims in the Frame. *Interventions*, 12(2),145–156. https://doi.org/10.1080/1369801X.2010.489687.

Morgan, M., & Shanahan, J. (2017). Television and the Cultivation of Authoritarianism: A Return Visit from an Unexpected Friend. *Journal of Communication*, 67, 424–444. https://doi.org/10.1111/jcom.12297.

MSN Entertainment. (2019). Rami Malek Won't Be a 'Stereotypical Arab Terrorist' in Bond Film. June 28. https://www.msn.com/en-ae/entertainment/celebhub/rami-malek-wont-be-a-stereotypical-arab-terrorist-in-bond-film/ar-AADyLgW. Accessed July 7, 2019.

Mulder, S. (2019). https://twitter.com/stephenniem/status/1152687057468317696?s=21.

Murrar, S., & Brauer, M. (2017). Entertainment-Education Effectively Reduces Prejudice. Group Processes and Intergroup Relations, 1–25. http://sohadmurrar.com/wordpress/wpcontent/uploads/2017/01/GPIR_MurrarBrauer2017.pdf.

Naber, N. S. (2014). Imperial Whiteness and the Diasporas of Empire. *American Quarterly*, 66(4), 1107–1115. doi: 10.1353/aq.2014.0068.

Nakayama, T. K., & Krizek, R. L. (1995). Whiteness: A Strategic Rhetoric. *Quarterly Journal of Speech*, 81, 291–309. https://doi.org/10.1080/00335639509384117.

Neale, S. (2004). Action-Adventure as Hollywood Genre. In Y. Tasker (Ed.), *Action and Adventure Cinema* (pp.71-83). New York: Routledge.

Nederveen Pieterse, J. (2001). *Development theory: Deconstructions / reconstructions.* London: Sage Publications.

Noakes, J. & Wilkins, K. (2002). Shifting frames of the Palestinian movement. *Media, Culture, and Society*, 24(5), 649-671.

Nossek, H., & Carpentier, N. (2019). Community Media, their Communities and Conflict: A Mapping Analysis of Israeli Community Broadcasting Groups. *Journal of Alternative and Community Media.* (online version).

Notley, T., & Dezuanni, M. (2019). Advancing Children's News Media Literacy: Learning from the Practices and Experiences of Young Australians. *Media, Culture & Society*, 41(5), 689–707. https://doi.org/10.1177/0163443718813470.

Ogan, C., Willnat, L., Pennington, R., & Bashir, M. (2014). The Rise of Anti-Muslim prejudice: Media and Islamophobia in Europe and the United States. *The International Communication Gazette*, 76(1), 27–46. https://doi.org/10.1177/1748048513504048

Oliver, M.B. (1999). Caucasian Viewers' Memory of Black and White Criminal Suspects in the News. *Journal of Communication*, 49(3), 46–60. https://doi.org/10.1111/j.1460-2466.1999.tb02804.x.

Ortiz, M., & Harwood, J. (2007). A Social Cognitive Theory Approach to the Effects of Mediated Intergroup Contact on Intergroup Attitudes. *Journal of Broadcasting and Electronic Media, 51,* 615–631. doi:10.1080/08838150701626487.

Pamment, J. . (2015). Strategic Communication Campaigns at the Foreign and Commonwealth Office: Managing Mediatization during the Papal Visit, the Royal Wedding, and the Queen's Visit to Ireland. *International Journal of Strategic Communication*, 9, 118–133. https://doi.org/10.1080/1553118X.2015.1008633.

Park, J., & Wilkins, K. (2005). Re-orienting the Orientalist Gaze. *Global Media Journal*, 4(6), Article 2.

Park, J., Felix, K., & Lee, G. (2007). Implicit Attitudes toward Arab-Muslims and the Moderating Effects of Social Information. *Basic and Applied Social Psychology*, 29, 35–45. http://dx.doi.org/10.1080/01973530701330942.

Pennebaker, J. W., Boyd, R. L., Jordan, K., & Blackburn, K. (2015). *The Development and Psychometric Properties of LIWC2015*. Austin: University of Texas at Austin.

Pew Research Center. (2017a). Demographic Portrait of Muslim Americans. http://www.pewforum.org/2017/07/26/demographic-portrait-of-muslim-americans/. Accessed September 29, 2017.

———. (2017b). World Muslim Population More Widespread Than You Might Think. http://www.pewresearch.org/fact-tank/2017/01/31/worlds-muslim-population-more-widespread-than-you-might-think/. Accessed September 29, 2017.

Pitter, L. (2017). Hate Crimes against Muslims in US Continue to Rise in 2016. Human Rights Watch, May 11th. https://www.hrw.org/news/2017/05/11/hate-crimes-against-muslims-us-continue-rise-2016. Accessed October 3, 2017.

Purnell, K. (2018). Grieving, Valuing, and Viewing Differently: The Global War on Terror's American Toll, *International Political Sociology*, 12(2), 156–171. https://doi.org/10.1093/ips/olyo04.

Rada, J. A., & Wulfemeyer, K. T. (2005). Color Coded Racial Descriptors in Television Coverage of Intercollegiate Sports. *Journal of Broadcasting & Electronic Media*, 49:1, 65–85. doi: 10.1207/s15506878jobem4901_5.

Reuters (2018). U.S. Anti-Muslim Hate Crimes Rose 15 Percent in 2017: Advocacy Group. April 23. https://www.reuters.com/article/us-usa-islam-hatecrime/u-s-anti-muslim-hate-crimes-rose-15-percent-in-2017-advocacy-group-idUSKBN1HU240. Accessed April 11, 2021.

Rockler, N. R. (2002). Race, Whiteness, "Lightness," and Relevance: African American and European American Interpretations of *Jump Start* and *The Boondocks*.' *Critical Studies in Media Communication*, 19(4), 398–418. https://doi.org/10.1080/07393180216569.

Said, E. (1978). *Orientalism*. New York: Pantheon Books.

———. (1997). *Covering Islam*. New York: Vintage Books.

Saleem, M., Prot, S., Anderson, C. A., & Lemieux, A. F. (2015). Exposure to Muslims in Media and Support for Public Policies Harming Muslims. *Communication Research*, 44(6). doi: 0093650215619214.

Sassan, S. (2006). *Territory, Authority, Rights: From Medieval to Global Assemblages*. Updated Edition. Princeton, NJ: Princeton University Press.

Scharrer, E., & Ramasubramanian, S. (2015). Intervening in the Media's Influence on Stereotypes of Race and Ethnicity: The Role of Media Literacy Education. *Journal of Social Issues*, 71(1), 171–185. https://doi.org/10.1111/josi.12103

Schmuck, D., Matthes J., & Paul, F. H. (2017). Negative Stereotypical Portrayals of Muslims in Right-Wing Populist Campaigns: Perceived Discrimination, Social Identity Threats, and Hostility among Young Muslim Adults. *Journal of Communication*, 67, 610–634. https://doi.org/10.1111/jcom.12313.

Schulz, W. (2004). Reconstructing Mediatization as an Analytical Concept. *European Journal of Communication*, 19(1), 87–101.

Schulzke, M. (2013). Being a Terrorist: Video Game Simulations of the Other Side of the War on Terror. *Media, War and Conflict*, 6(3), 207-220.

Sekarasih, L., Scharrer. E., Olsen, C., Onut, G., & Lanthorn, K. (2018). Effectiveness of a School-Based Media Literacy Curriculum in Encouraging Critical Attitudes about Advertising Content and Forms among Boys and Girls. *Journal of Advertising*, 47(4), 362–377. https://doi.org/10.1080/00913367.2018.1545269.

Selod, S. (2015). Citizenship Denied: The Racialization of Muslim American Men and Women post-9/11. *Critical Sociology*, 41(1), 77–95. https://doi.org/10.1177/0896920513516022.

Semaan, G. (2014). Arab Americans: Stereotypes, Conflict, History, Cultural Identity and Post 9/11. *Intercultural Communication Studies, 23(2),* 17–32.

Shah, H. (2003). "Asian Culture" and Asian American Identities in the Television and Film Industries of the United States. *Studies in Media and Information Literacy Education.* 3(3). http://www.utpress.utoronto.ca/journal/ejournals/simile doi: 10.3138/sim.3.3.002. Accessed September 28, 2005.

——. (2011). *The Production of Modernization: Daniel Lerner, Mass Media and the Passing of Traditional Society*. Philadelphia: Temple University Press.

Shah, H., & Wilkins, K. (2004). Reconsidering Geometries of Development. *Perspectives on Global Development and Technology*, 3(4), 395–416. doi: 10.1163/1569150042728893.

Shaheen, J. G. (2001). *Reel Bad Arabs: How Hollywood Vilifies a People.* New York: Olive Branch Press.

Sharp, J. M. (2009). U.S. Foreign Assistance to the Middle East: Historical Background, Recent Trends and the FY 2010 Request. Congressional Research Service 7-5700, July 17. https://fas.org/sgp/crs/mideast/RL32260.pdf.

Shen, C., Kasra, M., Pan, W., Bassett, G. A., Malloch, Y., & O'Brien, J. F. (2018). Fake Images: The Effects of Source, Intermediary, and Digital Media Literacy on Contextual Assessment of Image Credibility Online. *New Media & Society*, 21(2), 438–463. https://doi.org/10.1177/1461444818799526.

Sides, J., & Gross, K. (2013). Stereotypes of Muslims and Support for the War on Terror. *Journal of Politics*, 75, 583–598. doi: 10.1017/s0022381613000388.

Silverstone R. (2002). Complicity and collusion in the mediation of everyday life. *New Literary History*, 33, 745-764.

Šisler, V. (2008). Digital Arabs: Representation in Video Games. *European Journal of Cultural Studies*, 11, 203–220.

Slater, M.D., & Rouner, D. (2002). Entertainment-Education and Elaboration Likelihood: Understanding the Processing Of Narrative Persuasion. *Communication Theory*, 12, 173–191. doi:10.1093/ct/12.2.173.

Southern Poverty Law Center. (2017a). Anti-Muslim. https://www.splcenter.org/fighting-hate/extremist-files/ideology/anti-muslim. Accessed September 29, 2017.

———. (2017b). Hate Groups Increase for Second Consecutive Year as Trump Electrifies the Radical Right. February 15th. https://www.splcenter.org/news/2017/02/15/hate-groups-increase-second-consecutive-year-trump-electrifies-radical-right. Accessed February 16, 2017.

Statistica. (2015). *Film Industry in the US*. New York: Statistica, Inc.

Suwana, F. L. (2017). Empowering Indonesian Women through Building Digital Media Literacy. *Kasetsart Journal of Social Sciences, 38*(3), 212–217. https://doi.org/10.1016/j.kjss.2016.10.004

Tabbah, R., Chung, J. J., & Miranda, A. H. (2016). Ethnic Identity and Discrimination: An Exploration of the Rejection-Identification Model in Arab American Adolescents. *Identity*, 16(4), 319–334.

Tawil-Souri, H. (2012). It's All about the Power of the Place. *Middle East Journal of Culture and Communication*, 5, 86–95. doi: 10.1163/187398612X624418.

Telhami, S. (2019). How Trump's Approach to the Middle East Ignores the Past, the Future, and the Human Condition. Brookings, May 20. https://www.brookings.edu/blog/order-from-chaos/2019/05/20/how-trumps-approach-to-the-middle-east-ignores-the-past-the-future-and-the-human-condition/. Accessed June 3, 2019.

Toepfl, F. (2014). Four Facets of Critical News Literacy in a Non-democratic Regime: How Young Russians Navigate Their News. *European Journal of Communication*, 29(1), 68–82. https://doi.org/10.1177/0267323113511183.

Torreon, B. S. (2017). *Instances of Use of United States Armed Forces Abroad, 1798–2017*. Congressional Research Service 7-5700, October 12. https://fas.org/sgp/crs/natsec/R42738.pdf.

Torres, L. (2019). Nicolas Cage Says He Was Once on a Quest for the Holy Grail That Was Something Out Of "*National Treasure*." *Business Insider (Australia)*, August 8. https://www.businessinsider.com.au/nicolas-cage-new-york-times-holy-grail-dinosaur-skull-2019-8.

Tsaliki, L., Franonikolopoulos, C., & Huliaras, A. (2011). Making Sense of Transnational Celebrity Activism: Causes, Methods and Consequences. In L. Tsaliki, C.A. Frangonikilopoulos, & A. Huliaras (Eds.), *Transnational Celebrity Activism in Global Politics: Changing the World?* (pp. 297–311). Bristol, UK: Intellect.

Tukachinsky, R. (2015). Where We Have Been and Where We Can Go from Here: Looking to the Future in Research on Media, Race, and Ethnicity. *Journal of Social Issues*, 71(1), 186–199. doi:10.1111/josi.12104.

Tukachinksy, R., Mastro, D., & Yarchi, M. (2015). Documenting Portrayals of Race-Ethnicity on Primetime Television over a 20-Year Span and Their Association with National-Level Racial/Ethnic Attitudes. *Journal of Social Issues*, 71(1), 17–38. https://doi.org/10.1111/josi.12094.

——. (2017). Effects of Media Representations of Ethnic Minorities on Black and Latino Viewers' Self- and Majority-Group Perceptions. *Journal of Broadcasting and Electronic Media*, 61(3), 538–55.

Tully, M., & Vraga, E. K. (2018). Who Experiences Growth in News Media Literacy and Why Does It Matter? Examining Education, Individual Differences, and Democratic Outcomes. *Journalism and Mass Communication Educator*, 73(2), 167–181. https://doi.org/10.1177/1077695817706572.

USAID. (2015a). Egypt. http://www.usaid.gov/egypt. Accessed July 31, 2015.

——. (2015b). Iraq. http://www.usaid.gov/iraq. Accessed July 31, 2015.

——. (2015c). Jordan. http://www.usaid.gov/jordan. Accessed July 31, 2015.

——. (2015d). Lebanon. http://www.usaid.gov/lebanon. Accessed July 31, 2015.

——. (2015e). Libya. http://www.usaid.gov/libya. Accessed July 31, 2015.

——. (2015f). Middle East. http://www.usaid.gov/where-we-work/middle-east/. Accessed February 22, 2019.

——. (2015g). Middle East Regional Cooperation Program (MERC). http://www.usaid.gov/where-we-work/middle-east/merc. Accessed July 31, 2015.

——. (2015h). Morocco. http://www.usaid.gov/morocco. Accessed July 31, 2015.

——. (2015i). Syria. Accessed from http://www.usaid.gov/syria. Accessed July 31, 2015.

——. (2015j). Tunisia. Accessed from http://www.usaid.gov/tunisia. Accessed July 31, 2015.

——. (2015k). USAID: Who We Are. Accessed from http://www.usaid.gov/who-we-are/mission-vision-values. Accessed August 6, 2015.

——. (2015l). Yemen. Accessed from http://www.usaid.gov/yemen. Accessed July 31, 2015.

VGChartz. (2015). Yearly Chart Index. https://www.vgchartz.com/yearly/. Accessed June 30, 2015.

Voniati, C., Doudaki, V., & Carpentier, N. (2018). Mapping Community Media Organisations in Cyprus: A Methodological Reflection. *Journal of Alternative and Community Media*, 3(1), 17–32.

Watson, J., Selod, S., & Kibria, N. (2018). 'Let's Hope the Boston Marathon Bomber Is a White American': Racialising Muslims and the Politics of White Identity, *Identities*. doi: 10.1080/1070289X.2017.1397964.

Werbner, P. (2013). Folk Devils and Racist Imaginaries in a Global Prism: Islamophobia and Anti-Semitism in the Twenty-First Century. *Ethnic and Racial Studies*, 36 (3), 450–467. doi:10.1080/01419870.2013.734384.

Wilkins, K. (1995). Middle Eastern Women in Western Eyes: A Study of US Press Photographs of Middle Eastern Women. In Y. Kamalipour (Ed.), *The US Media and the Middle East: Image and Perception* (pp. 50–61). Westport: Greenwood Press.

———. (1997). Gender, Power and Development. *The Journal of International Communication*, 4(2), 102–120.

———. (2004). Communication and Transition in the Middle East: A Critical Analysis of US Intervention and Academic Literature. *Gazette: The International Journal for Communication Studies*, 66(6), 483–496.

———. (2008). *Home/Land/Security: What We Learn about Arab Communities from Action-Adventure Film*. Lanham: Lexington Books.

———. (2009). Mapping Global Space: Arab Americans and Others' Engagement with Action-Adventure Film. *International Communication Gazette*, 71(7), 1–16. https://doi.org/10.1177/1748048509341888.

———. (2012). Wearing Shades in the Bright Future of Digital Media: Limitations of Narratives of Media Power in Egyptian Resistance. *MedieKulture*, 28(52). http://ojs.statsbiblioteket.dk/index.php/mediekultur/article/view/5491.

———. (2015). Celebrity as Celebration of Privatization in Global Development: A Critical Feminist Analysis of Oprah, Madonna, and Angelina. *Communication, Culture & Critique*, 8(2), 163–181. https://doi.org/10.1111/cccr.12080.

———. (2016). *Communicating Gender and Advocating Accountability in Global Development*. Hampshire, UK: Palgrave Macmillan.

——. (2018a). The Business of Bilateral Branding. In J. Pamment & K. Wilkins (Eds.), *New Dimensions in the Politics of National Image and Foreign Aid: Communication, Development, and Diplomacy* (pp. 51–72). Hampshire, UK: Palgrave Macmillan.

——. (2018b). Communication about Development and the Challenge of Doing Well: Donor Branding in the West Bank. In F. Enghel & J. Noske-Turner (Eds.), *Communication in International Development: Doing Good or Looking Good?* (pp. 76–96). New York: Routledge.

Wilkins, K., & Downing, J. (2002). Mediating Terrorism: Text and Protest in the Interpretation of *The Siege. Critical Studies in Media Communication*, 19(4), 419–437. doi: 10.1080/07393180216571.

Willis, K., Smith, A., & Stenning, A. (2008). Introduction: Social justice and neoliberalism. In A. Smith, A. Stenning, & K. Willis (Eds.), *Social Justice and Neoliberalism: Global perspectives* (pp. 1–15). London: Zed Books.

Wilson, K. (2011). 'Race', Gender and Neoliberalism: Changing Visual Representations in Development. *Third World Quarterly* 32(2). doi: 10.1080/01436597.2011.560471.

Wright, L. (2006). *The Looming Tower: Al-Qaeda and the Road to 9/11*. New York: Knopf.

Xie, X., Gai, X., & Zhou, Y. (2019). A Meta-analysis of Media Literacy Interventions for Deviant Behaviors. *Computers & Education*, 139, 146–156. https://doi.org/10.1016/j.compedu.2019.05.008.

Yahya, M. (2019). The Middle East's Lost Decades: Development, Dissent, and the Future of the Arab World. *Foreign Affairs*, 98(6), 48–55.

Index

Founded in 1893,
UNIVERSITY OF CALIFORNIA PRESS
publishes bold, progressive books and journals on topics in the arts, humanities, social sciences, and natural sciences—with a focus on social justice issues—that inspire thought and action among readers worldwide.

The UC PRESS FOUNDATION
raises funds to uphold the press's vital role as an independent, nonprofit publisher, and receives philanthropic support from a wide range of individuals and institutions—and from committed readers like you. To learn more, visit ucpress.edu/supportus.

www.ingramcontent.com/pod-product-compliance
Lightning Source LLC
Chambersburg PA
CBHW030845270326
41928CB00007B/1233
* 9 7 8 0 5 2 0 3 7 7 0 2 8 *